FRENCH PILOT

PILOT

Volume One
Omonville to Tréguier

MALCOLM ROBSON

First published by
NAUTICAL PUBLISHING COMPANY LIMITED
Nautical House, Lymington, Hampshire, England

in association with
George G. Harrap and Company Limited London

March 1979

ISBN 0 245 53381 8

Caution
While great care has been taken in the compilation of
this book, it is regretted that neither author nor publisher
can accept responsibility for any inaccuracies or
mishaps arising from the work.

Filmset and printed in Great Britain by
BAS Printers Limited, Over Wallop, Hampshire

Contents

Introduction

Jagged headlands, savage tides, chunks of pink granite—that's Brittany. And Normandy?—Cathedrals miles up muddy estuaries banked with cider-apple trees. Is this your picture of the two dukedoms? Well, yes you're right—all this and more. But more contrasts. Like friendly rivers sheltering up steep valleys. Bustling fishing ports and tranquil anchorages. An hour away from a crowded marina you can be sharing a tiny quay with a pair of kingfishers.

The three hundred miles between Ile de Sein and Cherbourg give to British yachtsmen an ideal in cruising; harbours every few miles, interesting navigation, and all within a day's sail of the south coast of England. And what about all those cheeses, those wines, those 'fruits de mer'? And the welcome?—no paperwork, no officials and the smaller the place the warmer the reception, 'J'étais en Angleterre pendant la guerre, m'sieu'.

This guide is for he who wishes to cruise along the coast, up the rivers, among the islands and not—Grâce à Dieu—not the owner who uses his boat merely for transport. So if you are among those individuals whose habit is to make a beeline for Cherbourg, take the ebb down to St Peter Port, then belt across to Lezardrieux for a fortnight . . . this book is not for you. So why not buy a few French charts, fit legs to your boat and get a close-up of those entrancing places you have been seeing only through binoculars? Inside a week you'll be talking French and—if only in self defence—enjoying garlic. 'Every civilised man has two homelands' reminded Benjamin Franklin 'And one of them is France'.

The French treat electric supply as a jest, and sewage not at all, but when it comes to marking their coasts I know of no other country to equal theirs. The lights are numerous, the buoys enormous, the beacons prolific and anything with enough space carries its name in big letters. First class maintenance of the entire system is the year-round job of the Ponts at Chaussées baliseurs whose skippers incidentally are mines of information.

You won't find this a treatise on navigation; locating your position before looking for pilot marks is elementary coastal plotting. Also, since inflation is as sure as sunrise, costs haven't been mentioned. Nor does this pretend to be a restaurant guide; what was top last year may be a discothéque this. But if there is one thing I would most humbly beg you to accept advice about, it is . . . legs. Every fishing boat, every yacht, motor boat, in Normandy and Brittany, from 1 to 100 tons fits les béquilles. Less than one in ten of the harbours I describe doesn't dry, so without legs and a straight keel for taking the bottom, you might just as well save the cost of this book. Since they were built before divers, few older harbour walls project further than LAT, so you will just have to get used to berthing single-legged, either against a quay or another boat. In any port, naturally working fishing boats come first, so, often you will have to dry in mid-harbour using both legs. You will therefore need a ladder; either folding, made from rope, or rigid. My own home-made one is typical of thousands; it fits to a leg when dried out in the open; it hangs from a ladderless (therefore often vacant) part of a high quay; it's used for bathing; it is a gangplank.

Notice how sparing I am about amenities. Whether the banks open on Friday or Saturday seems of less importance than knowing there will be 4·1 metres in an hour alongside the quay.

Lobster pots need particular care since they have floats on long buoyant rope, to cope with the big tidal range. Often their owners lay them in narrow, rocky channels and with scant heed

4

to traffic. And from traffic so to transport. After years of cruising with collapsable bikes we now have folding mopeds. With either you will see something of rural France apart from quaysides, thus making those remote anchorages even more pleasant. What's worse than a two-mile heavily laden walk in the opposite direction to a café? Drinking water is seldom a bother and today even the tiniest quay has its water tap, perfectly pure, thanks to recent Government ordinances. Auto-laundrettes are worth a mention, as are showers; both are rare. But don't turn your nose up at public showers, which are cheap, hot and—quite unlike public lavatories—spotlessly clean.

Recent Customs changes now oblige pleasure boats to use fuel taxed at the same rate as road users, and as quayside pumps only provide low-duty fuel to fishermen, this can become a problem. If you can take enough you might persuade a small road tanker to deliver by hose, otherwise take your cans to the filling station. Fuel Oil Domestique is forbidden for yachts.

Unless you use the tiny but ubiquitous International Camping Gaz cylinders, bottled gas is another perennial headache. Nobody will exchange British containers and I know of no handy plant where they can be filled, so the best solution is to carry enough spare gas on board. Paraffin users will laugh coarsely at all this fuss—until they too have to gather a few sticks for cooking—their tipple is called 'petrole' and may be bought with increasing bother at paint shops.

Very many cruises seem to start somewhere around Cherbourg but not many British yachts reach Biscay, so I hope you will agree with my frontiers which are the two major headlands of Pointe du Raz and Cap de la Hague. Cherbourg has been left out; it is a vast port presenting few difficulties and even less interest. Information is arranged in sequence from north-east (Omonville) to south-west (Raz de Sein). For the sake of convenience the area has been divided about halfway into two books. The coverage of the sections for part I, A–C, is on Fig. 2. There is no overlap either in charts or marks, though the tidal and radio information is common to both books:

Part I—Omonville to Tréguier.

Part II—Port Blanc to Raz de Sein.

I must mention here that directions for the Channel Islands come in my sister volume *Channel Islands Pilot*.

Finally while information has been checked, sorted and rechecked, still errors can creep in, so neither the publisher nor I can be responsible for mistakes or omissions. But, please if you find any faults or you can supply additions, could you write to me in Sark?

Most of the marks have been sailed over in our 44 ft sloop *Hephzibah*.

5

Charts

Any mention of charts in this book refer to my sketch charts. The three areas A–C are in Fig. 2, detailed charts are indexed in Figs 3, 4, 5. Charts are metric and soundings, drying heights, elevations have been reduced to LAT. Liberties have been taken to envelop collective dangers and there are only three very basic contours . . . HAT, LAT and the 3-metre line. Anything below this can't be of great interest to yachts. In the text a figure in italics (e.g. *1·2m*) shows the height in metres drying out above chart datum (LAT). One big difference between French and British charts is in the height of rocks which never cover, but I've followed the Admiralty by showing heights as measured above MHWS. French charts instead give this as the height above chart datum (LAT). Headway under bridges is the same and I give this as above MHWS. Bearings are true; those of lights from seaward; of transits as seen in the view. Symbols are generally those on Admiralty Chart 5011, alas without colours, Fig. 1. Section that down the middle, and you have approximately Fig. 12. I very seldom show rocks—the area is wall-to-wall anyway—unless of significance. Their elevations I've guessed sometimes to point the difference between 20m and 5m; who cares if they really should be 17·8 and 5·3? Drying ground may contain rocks, sand, shingle, mud, or a mixture of the lot. Similarly the quality of the bottom is ignored; however no anchorages are shown in known poor holding.

Fig. 1. Key to chart symbols

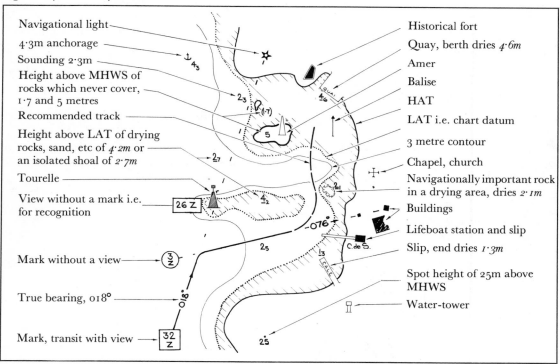

Navigational light
4·3m anchorage
Sounding 2·3m
Height above MHWS of rocks which never cover, 1·7 and 5 metres
Recommended track
Height above LAT of drying rocks, sand, etc of *4·2m* or an isolated shoal of *2·7m*
Tourelle
View without a mark i.e. for recognition
Mark without a view
True bearing, 018°
Mark, transit with view

Historical fort
Quay, berth dries *4·6m*
Amer
Balise
HAT
LAT i.e. chart datum
3 metre contour
Chapel, church
Navigationally important rock in a drying area, dries *2·1m*
Buildings
Lifeboat station and slip
Slip, end dries *1·3m*
Spot height of 25m above MHWS
Water-tower

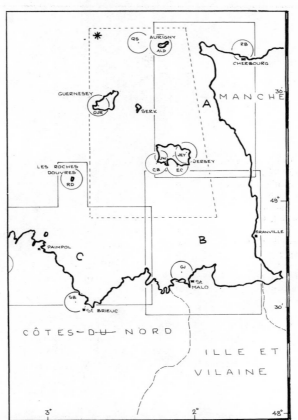

A   Manche

B   Baie de Mont St Michel

C   Baie de St Brieuc

* See 'Channel Islands Pilot'.

Fig. 2. Index to the book sections

Compass roses are absent, the side margins are true north. East margins show minutes of latitude and tenths i.e. nautical miles and cables. The south gives minutes and tenths of longitude. Where these are omitted I draw a scale. A cable = 185 metres = 608 feet. To give some clue to the terrain, spot heights are sometimes shown in metres above MHWS.

Stupid mistakes are inevitable in constantly changing from British to French charts; swapping from metres to feet; confusing abbreviations like B = black = blanc. Therefore my views and charts, abbreviations, colours, lights are all in French. My charts are never intended to substitute for proper navigational charts. But when you buy these, buy French because Admiralty coverage is meagre and the scales are small. Some 20 charts cover the same area as 75 French ones, which can be bought from most Admiralty agents in the U.K. and in many French ports. Keep them corrected from Notices to Mariners, clean, dry and flat for they cost double; Admiralty charts are indexed in Fig. 6, French small scale passage charts in Fig. 7. Larger scale detail French charts are shown in Fig. 8. From Fig. 2 you will note that areas A and B overlap into 'Channel Islands Pilot' a book of mine like this in format, method and description of marks, and therefore complimentary, since in this one I omit everything about the Islands.

French Pilot I

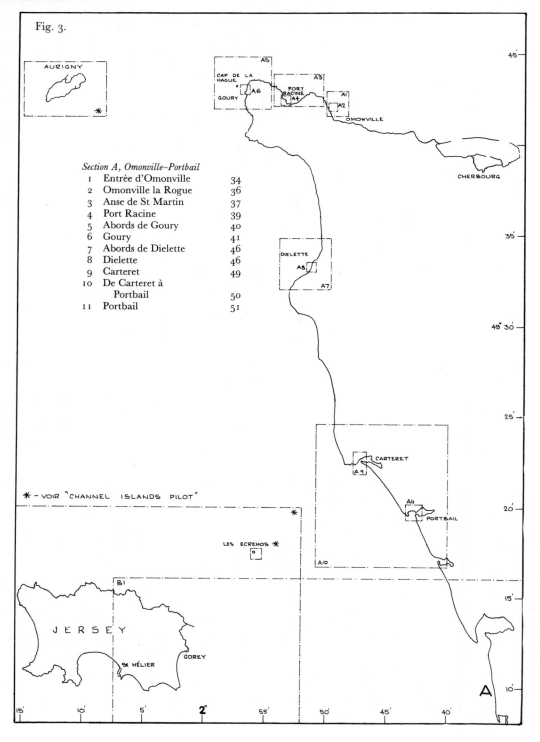

Fig. 3.

AURIGNY

✳

A5

CAP DE LA HAGUE

GOURY A6

PORT RACINE A4

A3

A1

A2

OMONVILLE

CHERBOURG

45'

35'

DIELETTE

A8

A7

49° 30'

25'

CARTERET

A9

A11

PORTBAIL

A10

✳ - VOIR "CHANNEL ISLANDS PILOT"

✳

LES ECREHOS ✳

B1

J E R S E Y

ST HÉLIER

GOREY

20'

15'

A

10'

15'   10'   5'   2°   55'   50'   45'   40'

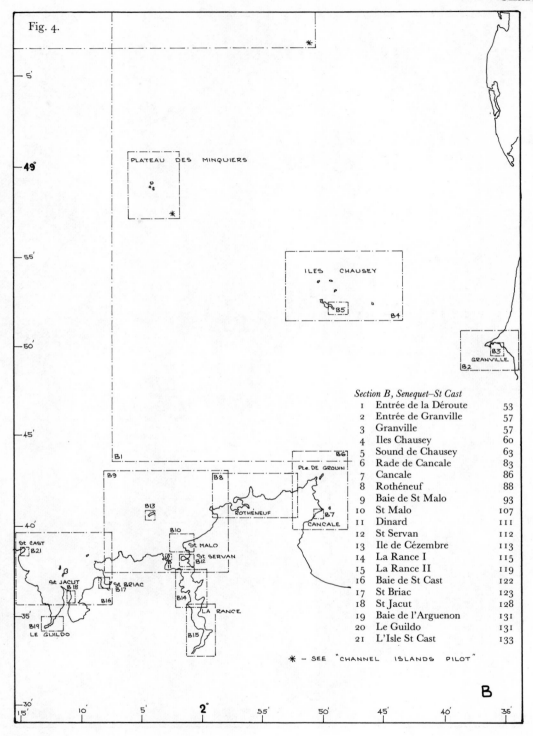

Fig. 4.

PLATEAU DES MINQUIERS

ILES CHAUSEY

B5

B4

B3

GRANVILLE

B2

B1

B6

Ple. DE GROUIN

B9

B8

B13

ROTHÉNEUF

B7

CANCALE

B10

St MALO

St SERVAN

B12

St CAST

B21

St JACUT

B18

St BRIAC

B17

B16

B14

LA RANCE

B19

LE GUILDO

B15

✻ – SEE "CHANNEL ISLANDS PILOT"

B

9

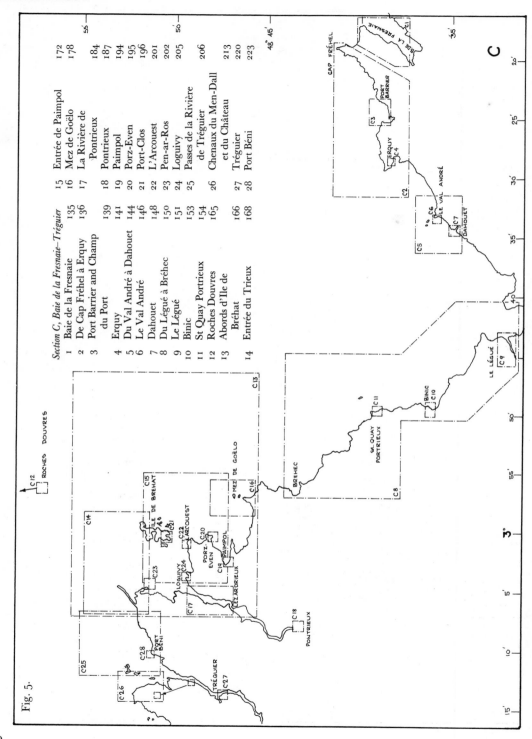

Fig. 5.

A single word, light, describes lighthouses, light beacons, light structures and the characteristic is given both on a chart and in a view. In thick weather or gathering dusk it is comforting to recognise quickly a beacon, light, which is why I have included so many of their profiles. A balise is a pole with a topmark, but if it's on a rock it might have a concrete base for strength. A tourelle is of masonry or concrete, commonly like a capsized flower pot and always with a topmark. It is promoted to a phare (lighthouse) if it is given a light. Amers, many of which are relics of an era before lights and uniform buoyage, are daymarks, more often white than coloured and very often form one of a pair of transit marks. They never carry navigational topmarks, are mostly in stone or concrete, look like slim pyramids or cylinders. Walls on land are mur-amers, very rare. Hang a light on an amer and it becomes a phare. Publications of the Service Hydrographique et Océanographique de la Marine with Admiralty equivalents are:

Catalogue-Index A, Europe et Méditerranée	4A	Catalogue of Charts, Home Edition	NP 109
Atlas des Courants de marée, Dunkerque à Brest	551	Tidal Stream Atlas, English and Bristol Channels	NP 250
Radiosignaux 1er Vol	191	List of Radiobeacons	NP 275(2)
Annuaire des marées Tome 1, France	5	Tide Tables Vol 1, Europe	NP 200
Feux et Signaux de Brume, Manche et Océan Atlantique est	C	List of Lights Vol A, Dunkerque to Brest	NP 74
		List of Lights Vol D, Eastern Atlantic	NP 77
Signes conventionnels and abbreviations	SH 88	Symbols and abbreviations	5011
Instructions Nautiques, France nord et ouest	C2	Channel Pilot	NP 27

French Pilot I

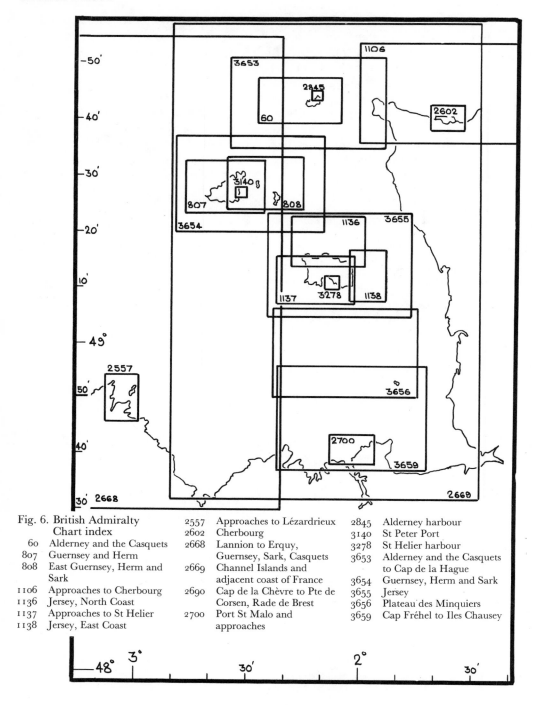

Fig. 6. British Admiralty Chart index

60	Alderney and the Casquets	2557	Approaches to Lézardrieux	2845	Alderney harbour
807	Guernsey and Herm	2602	Cherbourg	3140	St Peter Port
808	East Guernsey, Herm and Sark	2668	Lannion to Erquy, Guernsey, Sark, Casquets	3278	St Helier harbour
1106	Approaches to Cherbourg	2669	Channel Islands and adjacent coast of France	3653	Alderney and the Casquets to Cap de la Hague
1136	Jersey, North Coast	2690	Cap de la Chèvre to Pte de Corsen, Rade de Brest	3654	Guernsey, Herm and Sark
1137	Approaches to St Helier			3655	Jersey
1138	Jersey, East Coast	2700	Port St Malo and approaches	3656	Plateau des Minquiers
				3659	Cap Fréhel to Iles Chausey

Note: Pilotage directions for the Channel Islands are published in *Channel Islands Pilot*.

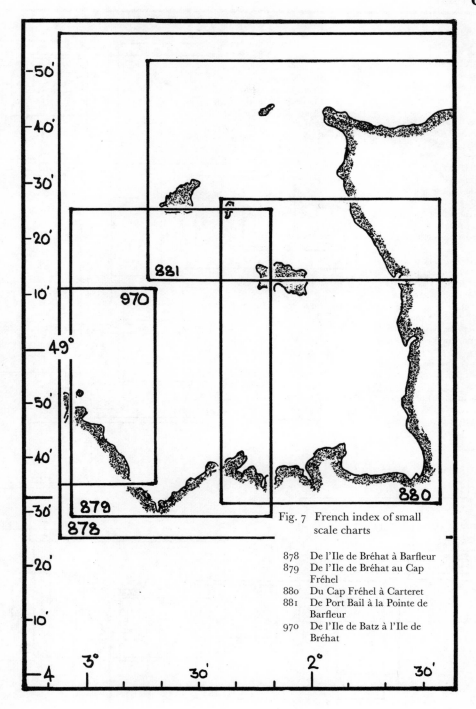

Fig. 7 French index of small
scale charts

878 De l'Ile de Bréhat à Barfleur
879 De l'Ile de Bréhat au Cap
Fréhel
880 Du Cap Fréhel à Carteret
881 De Port Bail à la Pointe de
Barfleur
970 De l'Ile de Batz à l'Ile de
Bréhat

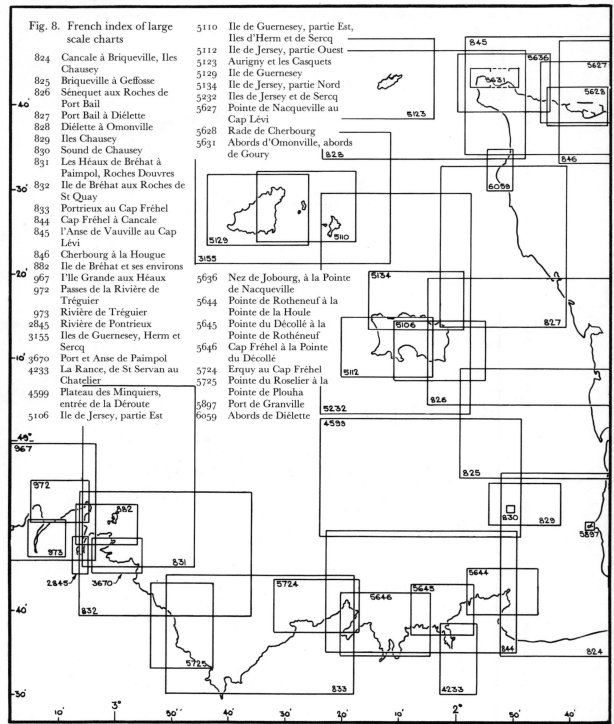

Fig. 8. French index of large
scale charts

824	Cancale à Briqueville, Iles Chausey
825	Briqueville à Geffosse
826	Sénequet aux Roches de Port Bail
827	Port Bail à Diélette
828	Diélette à Omonville
829	Iles Chausey
830	Sound de Chausey
831	Les Héaux de Bréhat à Paimpol, Roches Douvres
832	Ile de Bréhat aux Roches de St Quay
833	Portrieux au Cap Fréhel
844	Cap Fréhel à Cancale
845	l'Anse de Vauville au Cap Lévi
846	Cherbourg à la Hougue
882	Ile de Bréhat et ses environs
967	I'lle Grande aux Héaux
972	Passes de la Rivière de Tréguier
973	Rivière de Tréguier
2845	Rivière de Pontrieux
3155	Iles de Guernesey, Herm et Sercq
3670	Port et Anse de Paimpol
4233	La Rance, de St Servan au Chatelier
4599	Plateau des Minquiers, entrée de la Déroute
5106	Ile de Jersey, partie Est

5110	Ile de Guernesey, partie Est, Iles d'Herm et de Sercq
5112	Ile de Jersey, partie Ouest
5123	Aurigny et les Casquets
5129	Ile de Guernesey
5134	Ile de Jersey, partie Nord
5232	Iles de Jersey et de Sercq
5627	Pointe de Nacqueville au Cap Lévi
5628	Rade de Cherbourg
5631	Abords d'Omonville, abords de Goury
5636	Nez de Jobourg, à la Pointe de Nacqueville
5644	Pointe de Rotheneuf à la Pointe de la Houle
5645	Pointe du Décollé à la Pointe de Rothéneuf
5646	Cap Fréhel à la Pointe du Décollé
5724	Erquy au Cap Fréhel
5725	Pointe du Roselier à la Pointe de Plouha
5897	Port de Granville
6059	Abords de Diélette

14

Radio Beacons

These are shown on Fig. 2 as a circle with the identification letters inside. All are continuous.

Name	Type	Ident.	Frequency kHz	Emission	Range miles	Position N	S
CHERBOURG, FORT DE L'OUEST (1)	RC	RB	312.6	A2	20	49°40.5′	1°38.9′
ALDERNEY	Aero RC	ALD	383	Ao, A2	50	49°42.6′	2°11.9′
CASQUETS (2)	RC	QS	298.8	A2	50	49°43.4′	2°22.5′
GUERNSEY	Aero RC	GUR	361	Ao, A2	40	49°26.1′	2°38.3′
JERSEY, EAST	Aero RC	JEY	367	Ao, A2	75	49°13.2′	2°02.1′
JERSEY, WEST	Aero RC	JW	329	Ao, A2	25	49°12.4′	2°13.3′
CORBIÈRE	RC	CB	305.7	A2	20	49°10.8′	2°14.9′
ST HELIER, ELIZABETH CASTLE	RC	EC	287.3	A2	10	49°10.6′	2°07.5′
ST MALO, LE GRAND JARDIN	RC	GJ	294.2	A2	10	48°40.3′	2°04.9′
ST BRIEUC	Aero RC	SB	353.5	A1	35	48°32.6′	2°49.1′
ROCHES DOUVRES (2)	RC	RD	298.8	A2	70	49°06.5′	2°49.1′
ROSCOFF, BLOSCON	RC	BC	287.3	A2	10	48°43.3′	3°57.7′
ILE VIERGE (2)	RC	VG	298.8	A2	70	48°38.4′	4°34.1′
CRÉAC'H (3)	RC	CA	308	A2	100	48°27.6′	5°07.7′
ST MATHIEU (4)	RC	SM	289.6	A2	20	48°19.8′	4°46.3′
ILE DE SEIN (5)	RC	SN	303.4	A2	50	48°02.6′	4°52.0′

Several of the above stations are grouped in the following sequences with the beacons listed, at one minute intervals. Full details are in Admiralty List for Radio Signals—Vol 2 (NP 275–2).

(1)

Nab Tower	NB
Breaksea L.V.	BK
Cherbourg	RB

(2)

Eddystone	DY
Start Point	SP
Casquets	QS
Roches Douvres	RD
Ile Vierge	VG
Lizard	LZ

(3)

Eagle Island	GL
Mizen Head	MZ
Barra Head	BD
Round Island	RR
Tory Island	TY
Creac'h	CA

(4)

St Mathieu	SM
St Nazaire	NZ

(5)

Eckmuhl	UH
les Baleines	BN
Ile de Sein	SN
Pointe de la Coubre	LK
Ile de Groix	GX
Belle Ile	BT

Marks

Alignments, transits, lines, marks, they all mean one thing—a pair of objects one behind the other—which is all this book is about. Inshore pilotage depends entirely on marks, which word also describes a church, an amer, a house. A channel mark is when an alignment passes between dangers on both sides. A clearance mark keeps you away from dangers on one hand. A breast mark is secondary to a main mark, is roughly abeam, and usually tells when to turn, i.e. quit one mark and take another. How much to deviate from a mark, yet still be safe can only be judged from charts giving enough detail. Occasionally I have stressed one side or the other. The distant mark is given in the text before the nearer one; the sign '×' means 'by' to avoid confusion. A typical view is in Fig. 9—line 12Z a tower on a hill × a beacon on a rock. Sometimes the marks are not in dead alignment as when the dotted rear mark is opened. In Fig. 9 it is opened to the SW but to avoid any mistake I would write 'a tower to the right of a beacon on a rock'. This is safest when required instantly to change from an ahead to an astern transit. When going along using a stern mark, it is pointless and dangerous to look ahead only.

Fig. 9. Typical transit view

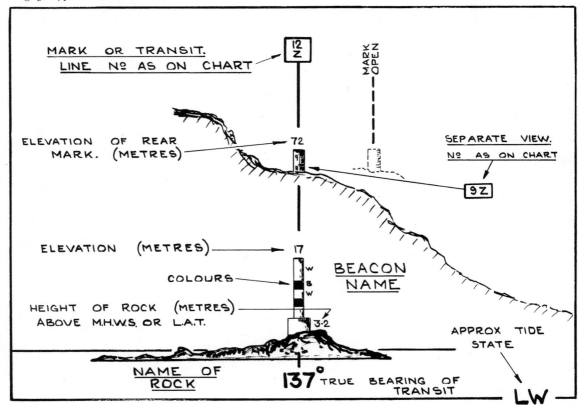

Make a check for lobster pots, other boats, etc. then turn and concentrate on the transit. Have ye no faith in my marks?

All the marks have been sailed or motored over, according to tide, in our 44 foot sloop *Hephzibah*; she draws 2·10 metres and from her decks, her cockpit, her crosstrees I have made the sketches. May I therefore quickly agree with all you art critics? But I'm a sort of seaman and not an artist; try struggling with wet paper, one hand on the chart and another on a bearing compass, binoculars under your arm, half an eye on the sounder, bellowing into a tape recorder—all at once. Then repeat the whole lot because it's too late for the tide, again since there's too much swell, or it's neaps instead of springs, better scrub it for today anyway for it's too misty to see the marks!

Perspective has been fiddled and detail omitted, both for clarity. If an object is framed, this shows that it is out of position. If of use I have sometimes shown the approximate tide level, but only LW, HT and HW, on average tides. Numbering of the lines is easy and I've tried to keep them in sequence. Charts are prefixed by the letter of their section (C1, C2, C3). Views in that section are suffixed by the same letter (25C, 26C, 27C). There are THREE kinds of transit numbers . . .

Within a SQUARE —A view with a transit on a chart, of the same number.
Within a RECTANGLE —A view of something, drawn large for recognition. The view may have a bearing.
Within a CIRCLE —A transit described in the text and on a chart, of the same number. There is no view, either because it is obvious, it isn't important, or there are no objects to make any marks.

Marks and Transit Lines

Glossary

Only words in the text and on charts are given. Breton names are in capitals. In this Celtic language letters are frequently interchanged, i.e. G–K–C'H, S–Z, G–W, B–V–P. An interesting dictionary of Breton-French is published by: Librairie de Finistere, 51 rue du Chateau, Brest 29N.

ABER	River mouth	Écluse	Lock
About	E.g. south-about is to set a course to leave an object to the north.	ENES, ENEZ	Island
		Épi	Spur of a quay
		EL, EN, ER	In the
Amer	Daymark		
Ancien, -nne	Disused, old	Feu	Light
Anse	Small bay, cove	Fosse	Ditch, channel
AR, AN, AL	The	FROUDE	Rapids
Balise	Perch, pole beacon	Gare SNCF	Station, French railways.
Basse	Low rock	GARO	Red deer
BAS, BAZ, BATZ	Shallow	Gateway	Course between two objects
Bec	Point		
BEG	Point	GLAS	Green
BENVEN, BOSVEN	High rock, stack	Goulet	Narrow entrance
BIAN, BIHAN	Little	Grève	Sandy beach
Blanc, -che	White	Gris, -e	Grey
Blanchi	White painted	Guérite	Small watch tower
Boue	Rock mostly submerged	GUEN, GUENN, GWEN	White
Bouée	Buoy		
BRAS, BRAZ	Big	Handrail	Passing around an object, or several on the one hand.
Brise-lames	Breakwater		
		HIR	Long
Cailloux	Gravel, stones		
Cale	Slip	KARREG, CARREC	Rock
C de G	Corps de Garde, watch house	KER	House, hamlet
C de S	Canot de Sauvetage, lifeboat station	KREAC'H, CREAC'H	Hillock
		KREIZ, CREIS	Middle
Chapelle, église	Chapel, church		
Château d'eau	Water-tower	LANN	Monastery
Cloche, Clocheton	Bell, turret	LEAC'H	Flat stone, place
Clocher	Steeple, belfry	LEDAN	Wide
Crossroads	Where two or more marks meet.		
		MARC'H	Horse
Damier	Chequered	MEZ	Seaward, wide
Demie	Half tide rock	MEAN, MEN	Stone, rock
Déversoir	Weir, spillway	MELEN	Yellow
Digue	Stone dyke	Méridional, -e	Southern
Dog-leg, zig-zag	Two courses parallel but offset, staggered.	MEUR	Great
		Mouillage	Anchorage
DU	Black	Moulin	Windmill, mill
Duc d'Albe	Mooring dolphin, pile	Musoir	Pierhead

Neuf, -ve	New	Rouge, RUZ, Rousse	Red, reddish
NEVEZ	New	ROZ, ROS	Wooded
Nez	Nose	Ruisseau	Rivulet, stream
Noir, -e	Black		
Nouveau, -elle	New	Sal Br	Signal de brume, fog signal
		Seuil	Cill, sill
Occidental, -e	Western	Sifflet	Whistle
Oriental, -e	Eastern	Son	Blast
		Sonde	Sounding
PEN	Head, headland		
Phare	Lighthouse	Terre plein	Levelled area near quay
Pierre	Stone	Tête	Head
Pignon	Gable	Tirant d'Air	Headway
Plat, -e, tte	Level, flat	Tirant d'Eau	Draught
PLO, PLOU, PLU	Parish	TOULL	Cave, hole
PORS, PORTZ, PORZ,		Tourelle	Navigational tower
Port	Harbour, inlet	Traverse	Intersecting channel
POUL, POULL	Roadstead, pool, lagoon	TREIZ	Passage
Presqu'ile	Peninsular	TREAZ, TREZ	Sandy
Raz	Race	Vanne	Sluice gate
Robinet	Tap	Vert	Green
Roche, ROC'H	Rock	Vieux, Vieille	Old
Rocher	High rock	VIR	Needle

Safety

France looks after her citizens who take to the sea by a system of licences for boats and examinations for skippers. There are some 20 weather forecasts daily (more in summer) and a list of times, frequencies and automatic telephones is given in a free leaflet 'la Meteo' from any Douane, Bureau du Port or Inscription Maritime. The leading shipping forecasts, with times used LOCALLY are:

Le Conquet (1673, 1876, 2691 kHz)—0833, 1733, 2253 hours, in French.
BBC (200 kHz)—0033, 0633, 1355 (1155 Sundays), 1755 hours.
Jersey Radio (1657·5, 1726 kHz, Ch 25)—0645, 1245, 1845, 2245 hours.

The equivalent to coastguard stations (of which the Channel Isles have none) are semaphores. These show storm warnings and are at prominent points:

> Goury
> Granville
> Pointe du Grouin, Cancale
> St Cast
> Ile de Bréhat
> Ploumanac'h
> Ile de Batz

RNLI lifeboats are stationed at St Helier and St Peter Port. French ones are at:

> Goury
> Granville
> St Malo
> Ile de Bréhat
> Ploumanac'h
> Ile de Batz

Tides

The predicted height of tide which you read in a tide table is the fruit of electronic soothsayers which digest data fed by coastal observers; they cannot take into account barometric pressure, prolonged wind from one direction, a storm surge, a seiche or a build-up on a sandbank. Then there is the personal element; swapping inches and feet for metres, looking up the wrong page, juggling with Greenwich, BST and French time. With all possible errors all going one way, the weather alone can alter the big tides of Normandy and Brittany by as much as 0·5 metre. So with all this in mind I have drawn, in Fig. 10, the tidal streams at twelve hourly intervals. Take care because, starting at half tide down, the streams only are timed with reference to St Helier, Jersey. These show the average conditions not on the hour shown, but approximately, during plus and minus half an hour. The rate of current is in tenths of a knot, the upper being springs, the lower neaps. N(il), N(ul) = zero current, slack water. HW, PM = high water, pleine mer. LW, BM = low water, basse mer. HT, MM = half tide, mi-marée. The scale of miles is on the top margin.

The second values on the diagrams are tidal. Against each of twelve places there is a square containing two figures which are the actual rise of tide, at that place (and not at St Helier) above its chart datum. The upper is the spring rise, the lower is neaps, given at the hour of each diagram and with reference to the times at that place. There's a reminder, if in doubt, which is neaps or springs, in the bi-lingual aide memoire at top left of each diagram. S(prings) are on top, N(eaps) at the bottom. V(ive) E(au) is above M(orte) E(au). Now how about a couple of examples?

(1) Southbound some 20 miles north of Ouessant I seem to be making slow progress. Why? First I reach for the Jersey tide tables and learn, at this moment it is $4\frac{1}{2}$ hours before St Helier high water and about halfway between neaps and springs. I look simultaneously at diagrams 5 and 6, locate where I am and jot down four figures. Springs, neaps, − 5 hrs, − 4 hrs = average 1·5 knots running about NNW, dead on my nose.

(2) It's a long while since I had a look at St Quay Portrieux, so I turn to Chart Index C, Fig. 5 and find chart C11. The cross berth near the Douane should be out of everybody's way; it dries 6·5m. What is the earliest on a rising tide, with my draught of 1·8m, that I can get alongside? First the St Quay Portrieux tide tables which say high water will be at 1815 this evening, height 10·9m. From simple inspection of the tide tables I learn that it is only a couple of days before springs. Then I reckon I must have at least 6·5m (the amount the berth dries) + 1·8m (my draught) = 8·3m rise. Now Portrieux is close enough to Binic to have the same rises, so I eye the top figures in the Binic square hopefully, say, on diagram 6, four hours before HW from which I see the rise is 3·0m—hopeless. Try the next (HW − 3 hrs) still not enough, 5·6m. But the next is just right (HW − 2 hrs) and the rise is 8·4m, slightly more than I need. So I can safely be tying up at 1815 − 2 hrs, or 1615—just nice time for tea.

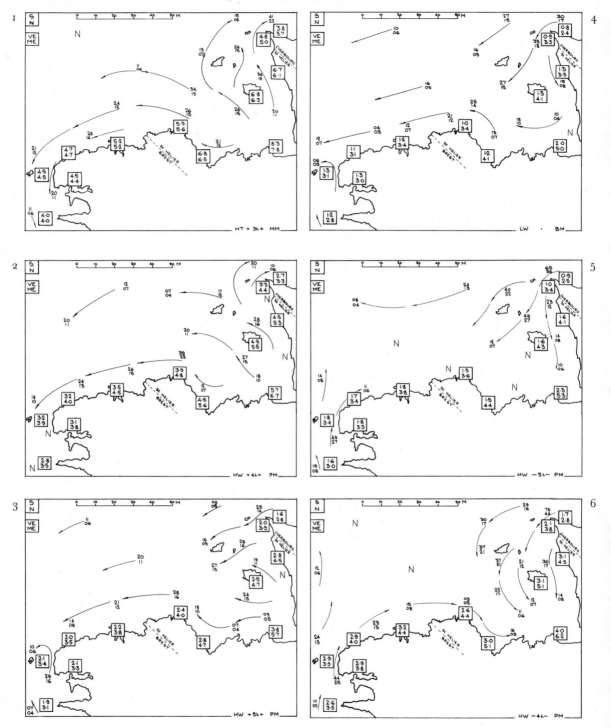

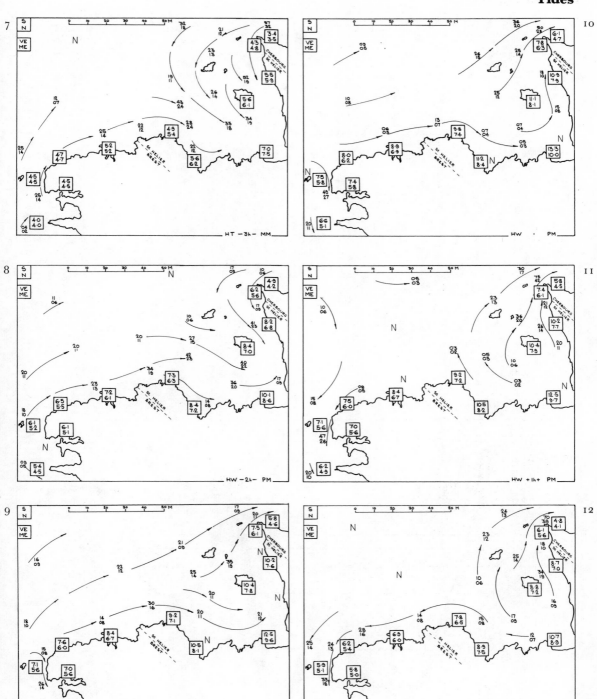

French Pilot I

	Heights								Ranges		Reference Port	G.M.T. Times at standard reference ports with differences	
	Astronomical tides		Mean Springs		Mean Neaps		Mean or half tide HT		Mean Springs	Mean Neaps			
	HAT	LAT	MHWS	MLWS	MHWN	MLWN						Springs	Neaps
Column	1	2	3	4	5	6	7		8	9	10	11	12
Cherbourg	6·8		6·2	0·8	4·8	2·3	3·5		5·4	2·5	Cherbourg	{ 0900 2100	{ 0300 1500
Omonville	6·7		6·1	0·8	4·7	2·4	3·5		5·3	2·3		−0015	−0020
Goury	8·5	Nil i.e. Chart Datum	7·8	0·9	6·3	3·3	4·6		6·9	3·0		−0057	−0110
St Helier	12·2		11·1	1·3	8·1	4·1	6·2		9·8	4·0	St Helier	{ 0800 2000	{ 0100 1300
Carteret	12·0		10·9	1·3	7·9	3·9	6·0		9·6	4·0		+0005	+0010
Cancale	14·6		13·3	2·0	10·0	5·0	7·6		11·3	5·0		−0005	−0013
Binic	12·3		11·2	1·2	8·4	4·1	6·2		10·0	4·3		−0032	−0033
les Héaux	10·7		9·8	1·0	7·4	3·4	5·4		8·8	4·0		−0030	−0024

Fig. 11. Tidal data for selected places.

Fig. 12. Tidal definitions

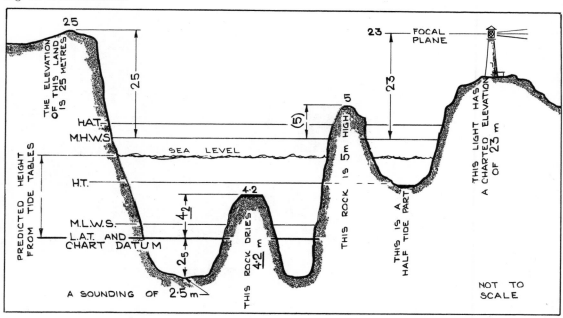

28

Tidal definitions are explained below, the columns refer to Fig. 11 on which are shown tabulated tidal data for the twelve selected places in Fig. 10.

HAT (Highest astronomical tide) **LAT** (Lowest astronomical tide) cols 1 and 2, are the levels which can be predicted to occur under average meteorological conditions and under any combination of astronomical movements.

MHWS (Mean high water springs) **MLWS** (Mean low water springs) cols 3 and 4, are the average rises throughout the year on two successive tides when the moon is at $23\frac{1}{2}°$ declination and the tide is greatest.

MHWN (Mean high water neaps) **MLWN** (Mean low water neaps) cols 5 and 6, are for the same conditions in cols 3 and 4 but when the tide is least.

HT (Mean half tide) col 7, is a convenient level used in areas with big tidal ranges. It is the average of cols 3 to 6.

RANGE, cols 8 and 9 is arithmetical. Cols 3–4 = 8. Cols 5–6 = 9.

TIME, cols 11 and 12 show the GMT of the spring and neap high water at the two standard ports in col 10, also the time differences of the 6 subsidiary places.

Dover is very approximately $4\frac{3}{4}$ hours AFTER St Helier. The above tidal definitions are graphically drawn in Fig. 12.

Just a reminder or so . . . BST, GMT or French time, but not a combination of all three . . . St Helier times for the currents only in Fig. 10 . . . local tide times for places near the squares, though . . . but make sure if the tide is rising or falling; the heights aren't always the same.

Buoyage

French buoyage is simple and consistent, and the daytime elements seen in this book are in Fig. 13 which also excludes wrecks and special marks. The three main divisions are Cardinal, Lateral and Isolated Dangers; all are alike whether for fixed or floating marks.

Dangers away from the shore or among rocks and islands use the Cardinal system. The bearing of the mark FROM the danger decides which of the four cardinal points to use. Memorising is vital, try . . . N is to the top of a chart, S is at the bottom, W is the letter on its side, E isn't. Note that French word ouest (west) is abbreviated on charts, etc to the English W. C.W. etc means Cardinal west, etc.

The Lateral system covers well defined channels, rivers and shows dangers alongside the route relative to the user. Isolated Danger marks are built on or moored over small limited dangers.

Whether it is a buoy, balise, tourelle or pierhead, it is the topmark which is the clue, which is why I have drawn in Fig. 13 dotted shapes, which vary considerably in practice. There are some 250 lights and lit buoys, too many, I'm sorry to say, to catalogue. When the French buoyage is harmonised with the IALA only small changes will be necessary; broadly it will scrap Transition, Bifurcation and Middle Ground marks. Abbreviations:

Éclat	É	Flash
Épave	W	Wreck
Fixe	Fixe	Fixed
Occultation	Occ	Occulting
Scintillant	Scint	Quick flashing

Fig. 13. French buoyage system

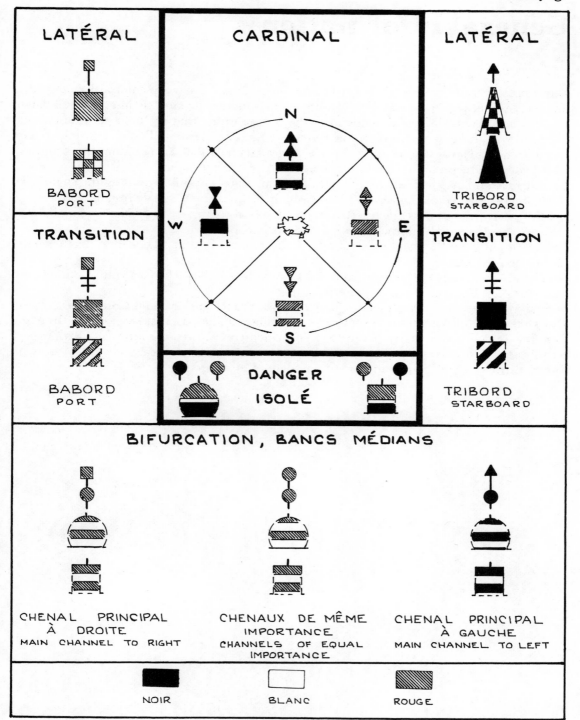

LATÉRAL

BABORD
PORT

TRANSITION

BABORD
PORT

CARDINAL

N

W   E

S

DANGER
ISOLÉ

LATÉRAL

TRIBORD
STARBOARD

TRANSITION

TRIBORD
STARBOARD

BIFURCATION, BANCS MÉDIANS

CHENAL PRINCIPAL
À DROITE
MAIN CHANNEL TO RIGHT

CHENAUX DE MÊME
IMPORTANCE
CHANNELS OF EQUAL
IMPORTANCE

CHENAL PRINCIPAL
À GAUCHE
MAIN CHANNEL TO LEFT

NOIR   BLANC   ROUGE

General Information

Customs. Pleasure boats arriving in France from abroad may only enter at a port with a douane, must have ships' papers, crew list and stores inventory, must fly international day or night signals. With whimsical Gallic logic they go on to say that by 'tacit declaration' and provided you arrive by sea, don't trade, run immigrants or charter to French citizens, you are free to come and go as you please. They can, and sometimes do, take a random check and can board your boat within 20 miles of the shore.

Immigration. Passports only, required but seldom asked for, unless quitting the country by some other route. You will need them for cashing cheques and for poste restante mail.

Health. Certificates not required. If you need medical treatment in France see the Foreign Office leaflet 'Essential Information for U.K. passport holders'.

Pets. Crippling fines if you bring a mammal back to the U.K. and practically a death penalty in the Channel Islands.

Money. Credit cards everywhere and all banks cash travellers cheques with no limit. You mustn't take away more than 5000 Frs in notes.

Security. I've never locked my boat in any part of France and see no reason to start.

Duty Free. Can be bought wherever there is a willing chandler in a customs port. You must get from the douane a free yearly 'green card' for which you will require a British Certificate of Registration. Duty-frees can be consumed in harbours as well as at sea.

Speed Limits. 5 knots under motor within 300m of the shore.

Acknowledgements

Unaided, no single person could possible write a book like this. Fishermen, pilots, yachtsmen, commercial skippers, all have given their local know-how, a piece here, a tip there, perhaps a warning. But more particularly I'm going to thank you patient Frenchmen without whom the job could have never even been launched—à votre santé—Capt Georges Bihannic, Capt Jacques Cadran, Capt Louis Lecoublet, Charles Frédouët, Gilbert Hurel, Louis Perouas, Commandante Richard Winter. Devils for punishment too, are John Lintell and Peter Procter, longtime crew in *Hephzibah*.

Most special thanks must go to my wife, Merrill Lyle, who as before did the note-taking and checking, the steering and sounding . . . as well as the charming.

My sketch charts and other information are based on Admiralty charts with the sanction of the Controller, HM Stationery Office and of the hydrographer of the Navy; and on French charts with the permission of l'Ingénieur Général de l'Armement, Service Hydrographique at Océanographique de la Marine. I am most grateful for the help of these two Government departments.

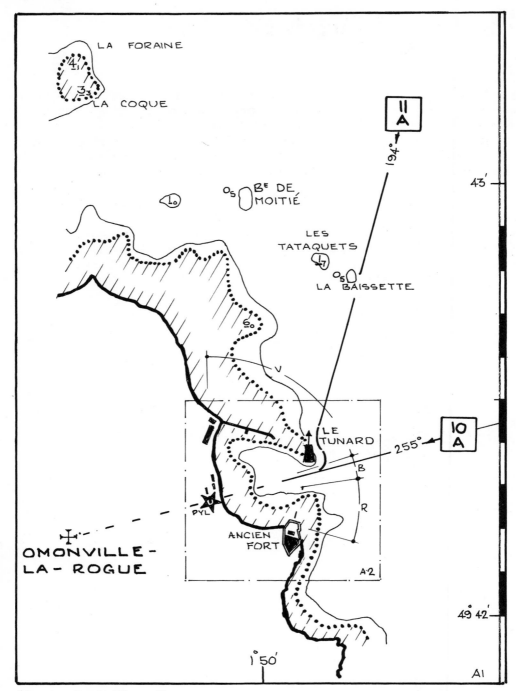

Chart A1—Entrée d'Omonville

A   Omonville to Portbail

OMONVILLE

Pentland Firth, Portland Race, you name it, wherever you sail there lurks the same dragon. That race where vast liners are turned end for end, these overfalls where trawlers vanish with monotonous regularity. Alderney Race—Raz Blanchard—is well to the top of the Big League for it runs a genuine 10 knots on the flood. But, as always, the secret is to find yourself there at the right time. Only the very foolish would elect to stand still for 4 hours in the middle of this 7 mile channel waiting for the current to slack off. If you know of some powerful prayers try belting down towards Guernsey with an 8 knot tide under you, against a brisk south westerly breeze.

Let's assume, then, we are westgoing and don't want to call at Alderney, so try and arrive a mile or so north of Cap de la Hague about when the SW-going ebb starts, St Helier + 5 hours, i.e. slack water. If you arrive too late, there are two small harbours just to the east; Omonville (4 miles) and Port Racine (2 miles). Both offer good anchorages though Omonville is better for drying out.

Chart A1 shows the entrance to Omonville and coming in from Cherbourg, look for the chapel—the only one in this granite village— × a new steel light structure, line

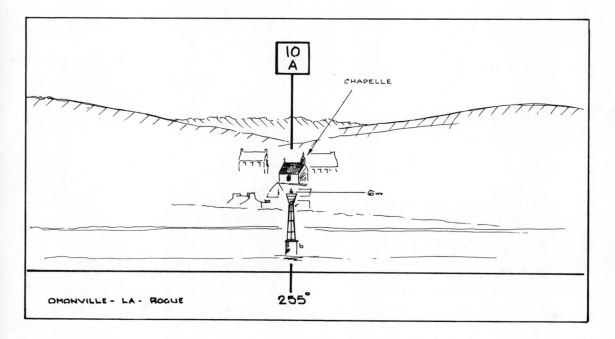

OMONVILLE - LA - ROGUE

255°

10A   which clears everything. By night use the white sector of the light. If arriving from the west you would clear outside the Basse Brefort (CN) buoy until line (11A)

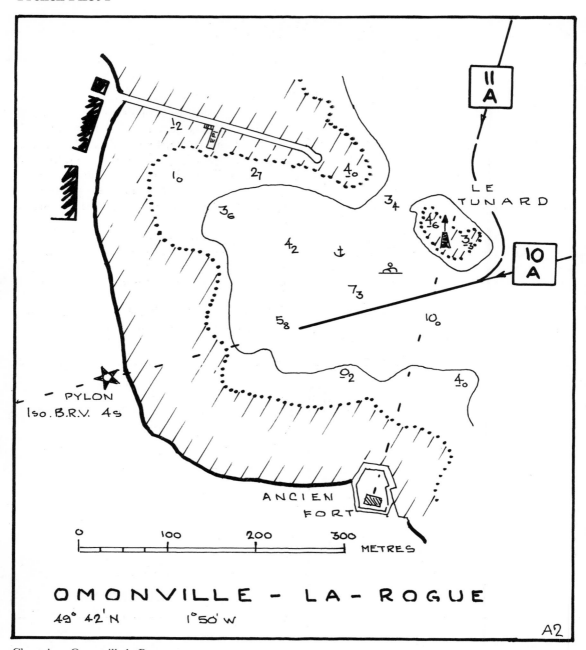

Chart A2—Omonville la Rogue

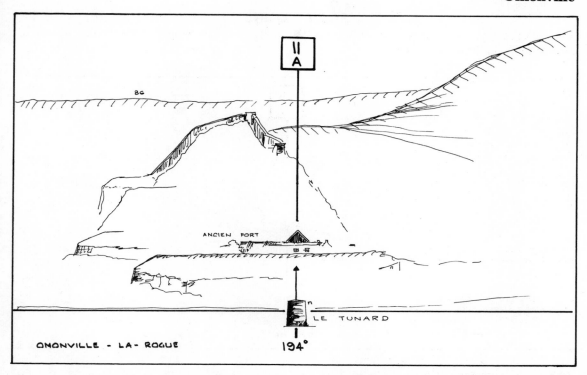

11A comes up. Some enterprising chap has used the parade ground of the old Fort d'Omonville for a house site, and his gable lines up with le Tunard tourelle. Don't try to pass north but leave this tourelle 75m to stb'd and join 10A as p. 35, see chart A2. There are one or two heavy naval mooring buoys in the anchorage. If you decide to dry out alongside, only the inner half of the jetty is usable. East of the south spur is all rock drying as much as *4m*. The best berths are about the *1·2m* drying figure. Restaurant, tap on quay, village shop 800m, fuel at garage.

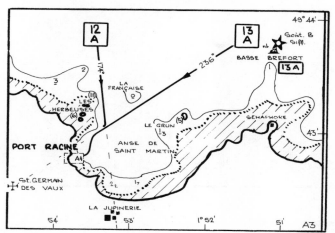

Chart A3—
Anse de St Martin

PORT RACINE

Chart A3 (p. 37) shows Anse de St Martin, a bay sheltered, surprisingly, from the east as well as from the prevailing winds. Line

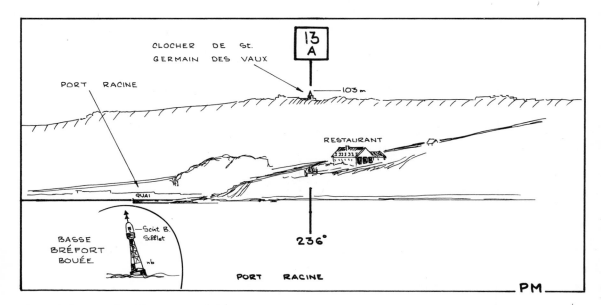

13A　　　clears both the shoals to the SE as well as la Française, one of a large patch in mid-bay. It is St Germain des Vaux spire × the left of Port Racine restaurant.

　　Between la Française plateau and les Herbeuses (11 to 6m high) is

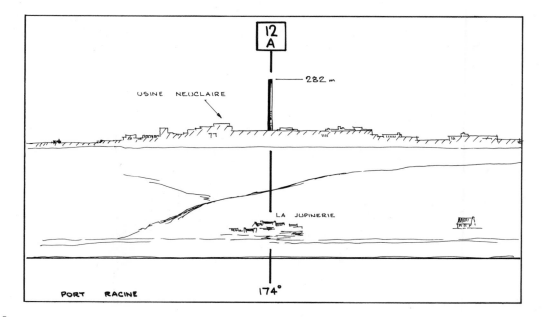

12A   the enormous chimney of the Atomic Research Station × a group of farm buildings. This chimney carries many obstruction lights (Fixe R) so with care may be used at night using the bearing on 12A. The best anchorage in the Anse is to get as far south as water permits, opposite la Jupinerie.

'The smallest harbour in France' reads a notice near the restaurant (I know a smaller near Brest), so before sweeping into Port Racine take a closer look at the scale on chart A4. Inside it is all level sand and about the size of a swimming pool. Apart from the restaurant, there isn't anything better than a kilometre walk to St Germain's village shop.

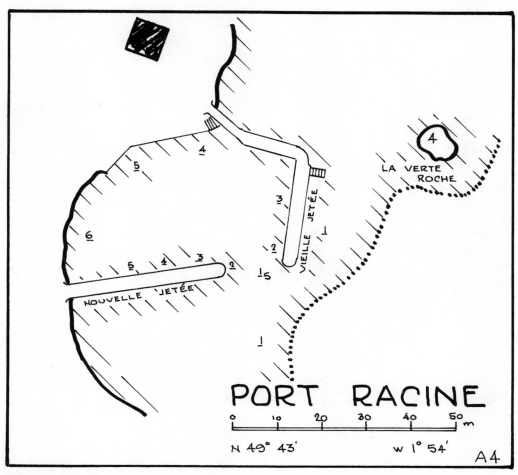

Chart A4—Port Racine

GOURY

Now how about sailing north-east through the Race? Instead of the above two convenient waiting rooms on the north coast, there is an inhospitable stretch of west-facing coast offering only Dielette 11 miles southward. Until you look closer at a large scale chart, that is, so here are two alternatives if you are caught out on the tide in the Alderney Race. Goury and le Haize Chenal, see chart A5.

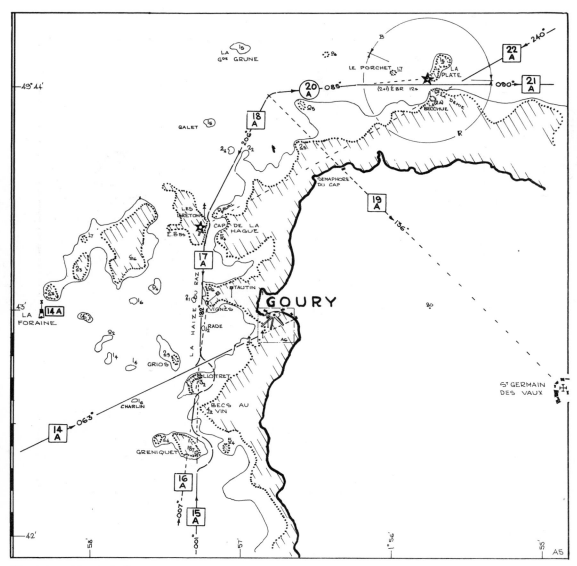

Chart A5—Abords de Goury

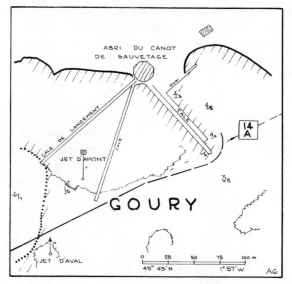

Chart A6—Goury

Goury is a harbour in its own right, not just a waiting stage. It has a single simple approach, see chart A6,

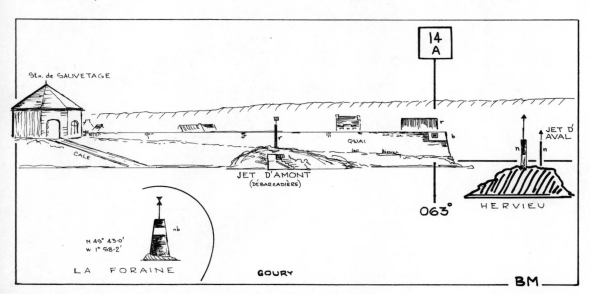

14A   the right side of a red roofed house × the white patch on the jetty end. This patch encloses a red square and the line leaves Charlin, 1·6m 50m to stb'd, les Grois, *2·9m*, to port, Liotret, 3·2m high, to stb'd, Hervieu and Jet d'Aval both to stb'd 10m. There is a buoy for the use of the adjacent lifeboat in 1·7m as shown on chart A6 and several other moorings westward. I have passed comfortable nights at anchor here in moderate SW winds and the lifeboatmen swear that even in gales the river of tide in the race acts as a breakwater.

French Pilot I

One or two fishermen only use the harbour, and it is level sand/mud; a good drying berth is about the *4·6m* sounding. There is a cafe/restaurant and it is only a km walk to the village shops in Auderville. The lifeboat station, the first in France to be motorised, has unique launching arrangements. Inside the octagonal building the boat rests on a turntable which serves either the high-water SE slipway or the low-water SW one. There are LW landing steps alongside the Jet d'Amont balise.

The second alternative, sailing north, is the inside channel, la Haize du Raz. This is a fascinating short-cut much used by local trawlers and its use is threefold. (a) When the Alderney Race looks like a clip from Dante's 'Inferno' there is hardly a ripple inside that mile long jumble of rock surrounding the lighthouse. (b) If you are just too late arriving at the Race before the SW ebb has started, you can cheat going northward in almost slack water. (c) It is the only way to reach Goury on the top of a NE flood tide, unless you have more than 15 knots under your hand.

The channel really starts close to the coast and south of Greniquet on chart A5 (p. 40) and even from a mile away the first mark

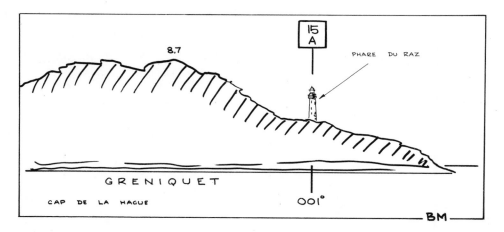

15A is seen, the lighthouse just to the right of Greniquet 8·7m high. When 50m off this monster rock, make a handrail eastabout until

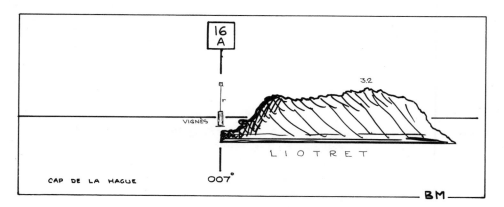

16A les Vignès balise is seen to the left of the only rock of its size, Liotret 3·2m high. Hold this transit only for a couple of cables until 50m off Liotret. Make a second handrail to the east until the stern mark

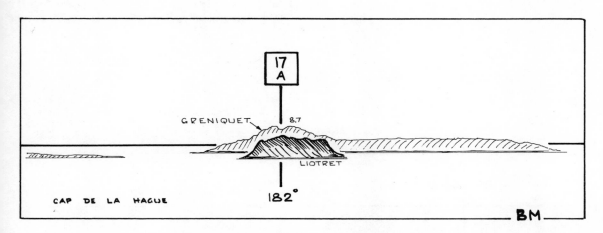

17A summits of Greniquet and Liotret are in line. You are now crossing the Goury entrance transit, but since we are continuing north this same mark serves for another half mile. Take a few seconds and glance seaward, listening to the roar of the ebb a short mile away. When within about 40–50m from the lighthouse quay, wave to the astonished keepers and borrow slightly to the east, say about 30m from the quay and the rocky steep-to base of the lighthouse islet. Leave les Brétons balise (CN) a scant 20m to port and get on stern transit

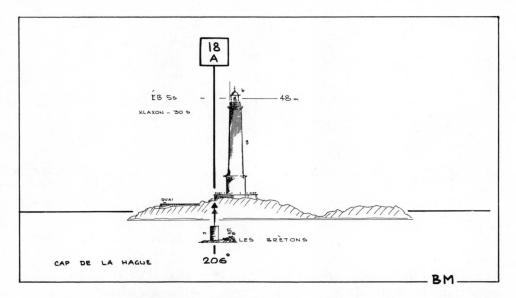

18A the left side of the lighthouse platform (it has railings) × les Brétons balise. Hold this stern mark for 6 cables, until a breast mark (19A)

43

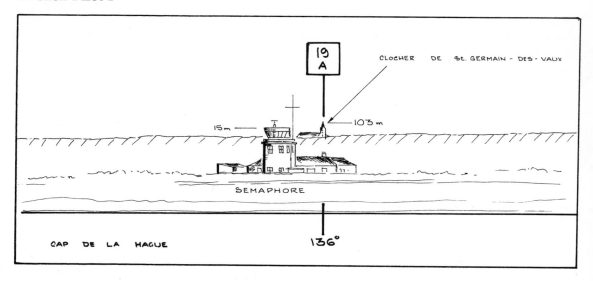

19A St Germain des Vaux church × the Semaphore du Cap. Quit the last mark and steer

20a (No view) 085° on la Plate lighthouse. I'm sorry no mark offers, but it is important to keep north of a *0·5m* rock near the turn. As soon as possible edge northward until

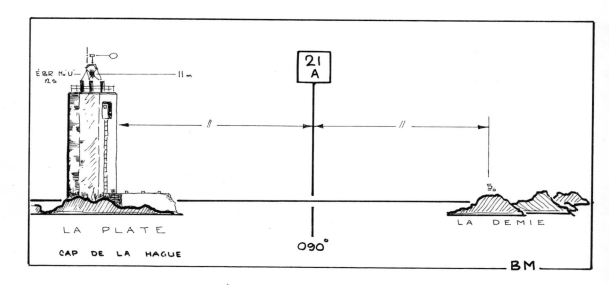

21A which is straight east halfway between la Plate and la Demie. In the unlikely event of la Demie being covered make it 40m from la Plate. The channel is 6m deep and over 100m wide.

And that's it. If you want to get away seaward, take

44

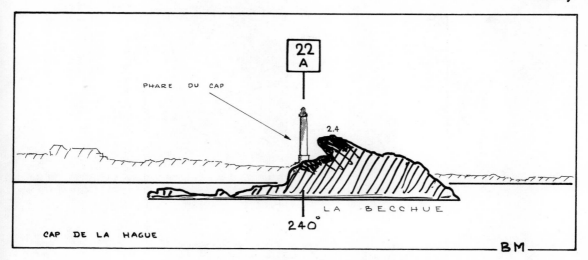

PHARE DU CAP

2.4

LA BECCHUE

240°

CAP DE LA HAGUE

22
A

BM

22A   the lighthouse of Cap du Raz × la Becchue 2·4m high, which clears to the south of a group of rocks NE of la Plate, la Ronde *1·5m*.

Although la Haize du Raz channel can be used for both directions it is going north where the gain is gainest. Taking it at springs, for example, when the Race is pouring to the SW at 8 knots (St Helier − 4 hours) the southward current in the Haize is 1·1 knots only. At St Helier − 3 hours it is slack and from then until St Helier + 5 hours it flows north east. At an hour after St Helier HW you have 5·2 knots in your favour. The maximum south-going current between Goury and the Raz lighthouse is 2 knots, at about LW. These are a third less at neaps.

Even on the full ebb when the current in the Race was 8 knots or more did you meet much above 1½, and that only close to la Plate? From Greniquet to la Plate is 2½ miles and the minimum depth is 2m, or 3·2m on the bottom of a normal spring tide.

If you want to carry on to Cherbourg, still against the west-going ebb, use the inshore eddy, from la Plate eastward. Maintain 270° on the gap south of la Plate for perhaps another half mile then steer to pass south of the Basse Bréfort. This is a 'big ship' buoy so leave it 2 cables to port and from there onwards don't stray more than a mile from the coast.

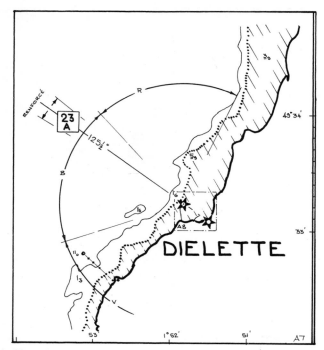

Chart A7—Abords de Dielette

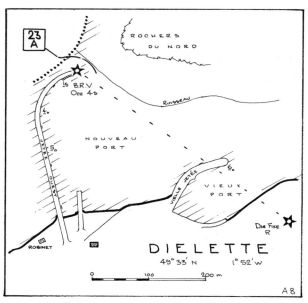

Chart A8—Dielette

46

DIELETTE

Back now to the south side of the Race, and the high cliffs of Jobourg, Flamanville and Carteret. On chart A7 is Dielette, a magnificent harbour albeit just drying, but alas without much to offer except shelter. The entrance is on chart A7, with one easy mark

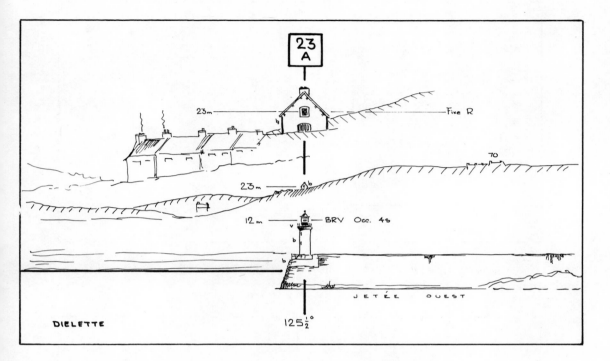

DIELETTE

23A the two lights in line. The rear light is unmistakable, it is the only white house with a gable, showing near the bearing. By night keep just south of the red sector of the front light when close in, see chart A8. There is a million pound jetty built out of cut granite blocks—a survival of a once prosperous iron ore port. The rusting remains of a telpher loader lie a mile southward. Ashore, armed and bored security men watch giant rock-movers munching away at the uranium-rich mountains.

CARTERET

Carteret, where the cliffs end and the thirty miles of dunes as far as Granville begin, is on chart A10 (p. 50). The approach is from the south, along line

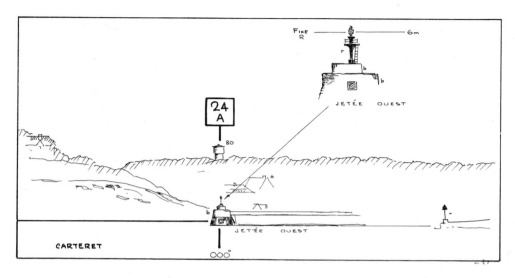

24A   the water-tower × the light on the end of the jetty. Chart A9 shows the harbour and when a cable off the light, change to line

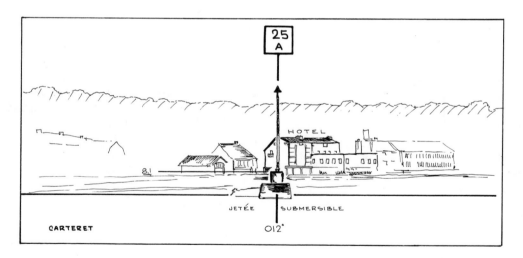

25A   the west gable of an hôtel × the stb'd balise on a submersible jetty. This line avoids a steep sandbank below the jetty light; and now to get the best possible water, count the old cannons embedded in the jetty on your port hand. There are four. At the first, edge toward the quay. From the second to the fourth, keep parallel and 15m from it. At the fourth come away and take a mid-channel course between the submersible jetty and the quay.

48

If the concrete base of the stb'd balise is awash, you have 2·2m of water as far as the Gare Maritime.

Most of the dozen fishing boats lie just upstream of the Gare Maritime, but a convenient berth can be found alongside the *6·1m* part. The Port de Refuge dries *9·0m*, good berths alongside, or you can carry on NE of the Terre Plein where there are drying marina moorings. The whole harbour is sand/gravel.

Since the quay has lights throughout its length, you can, with care, make a night entry using the Fixe R. jetty light with a bearing of 000°, then guessing the remainder. There is a Scint., B. light on the stb'd balise, unreliable.

Carteret is really the port of Barneville, a small town of some 5,000 and 3km inland, but all fuel, food and engine repairs are near the quays. Barneville has an interesting fortified 11th century church. In summer ferries run to Gorey (Jersey), Sark and St Peter Port (Guernsey). Showers at hotels, tap on quay.

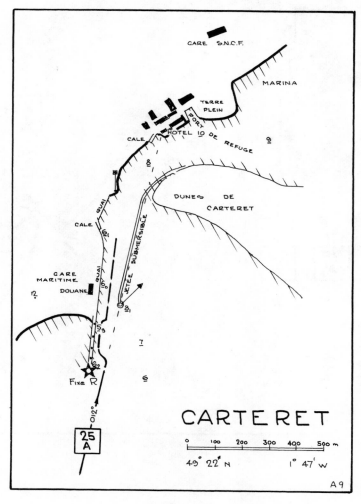

Chart A9—Carteret

49

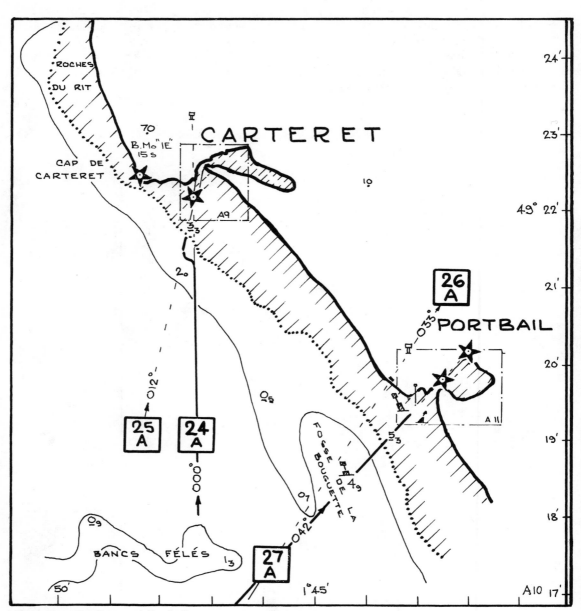

Chart A10—De Carteret à Portbail

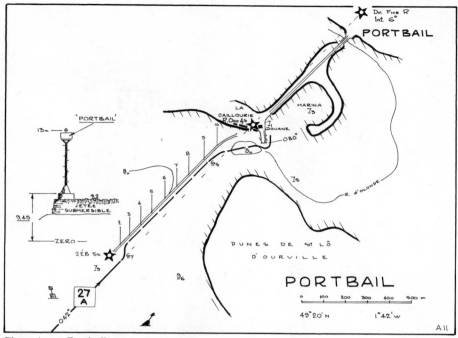

Chart A11—Portbail

PORTBAIL

Four miles southward is Portbail, chart A10. This is such a featureless coast that an aid to location is no bad thing, so I show line

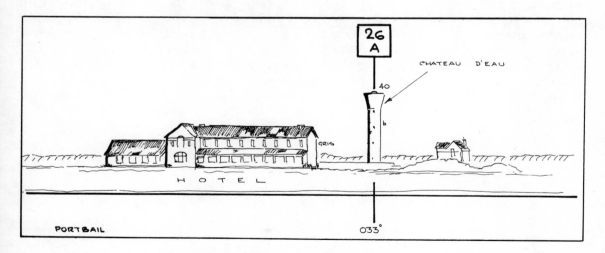

26A   a most conspicuous water-tower × a modern hôtel, which is only half a mile north of the entrance to Portbail, chart A11. The back mark of (27A)

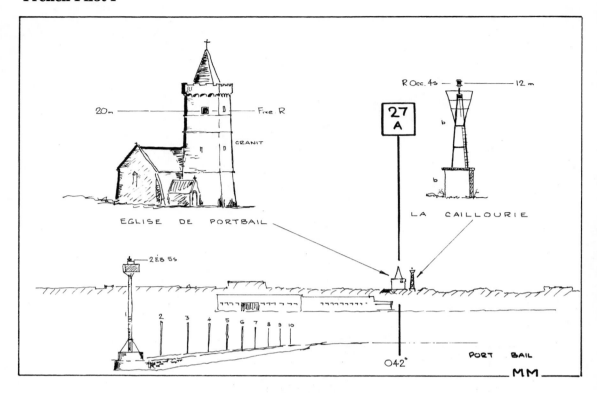

27A is hard to find, a squat grey granite church. Most economically, the back light occupies a window cut in the tower. Put this in line with la Caillourie. When abreast of the lit balise at the SW end of the submersible jetty, steer closer to the jetty, marked by a line of 10 posts and continue parallel and no more than 15m off. I have given these posts imaginary numbers and when abreast of No 9 steer 080° toward the southern end of the slip. The ferry skippers reckon that when the concrete base of the balise-light is awash (see chart A11) there is never less than 3m throughout the channel. The drying berths are on the east side of the slip marked 'Douane' and also in the 7·3m drying marina.

The village of Portbail is medieval in appearance, with a 15th century fortified church. Restaurants, garage, food shops; and showers at the Centre Nautique.

B Sénéquet to St Cast

LA DÉROUTE TO GRANVILLE

I have been sailing along the coast of West Normandy for many years and I treat it with increasing respect. Between Cap de la Hague and Granville is almost 60 miles of normally dead lee shore. There are no islands to shelter behind, no deep estuaries and between Jersey and France lie 10 miles of shoals. Not quite the area to be sailing, say in late October . . . darkness falling and so is the barometer . . . wind backs to the west and starts to pipe up . . . tide falling and all the harbours dry completely. Beat out to the west? Sark?—too difficult after dark. Alderney? if you feel up to all those currents. Guernsey?—what, 30 miles off? Jersey?—Yes, St Catherine but don't tangle with les Ecrehos. Chausey? well, if you must.

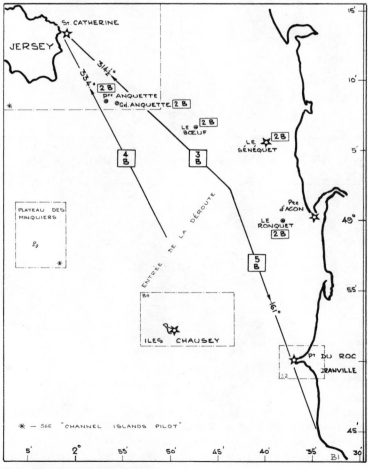

Chart B1—Entrée de la Déroute

53

However, let's assume that it's good visibility and you are sailing from Jersey to Granville, and here are two long-distance marks to take you safely through the reefs. They will serve equally well if approaching from the north, Carteret or Portbail. The body of water between Jersey, Sark and France is loosely called la Déroute, see chart B1 (p. 53)

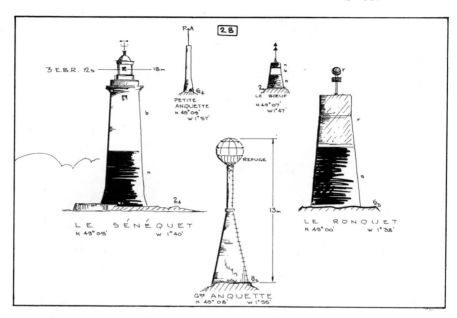

2B   shows portraits of five of the beacons you might wish to recognise.

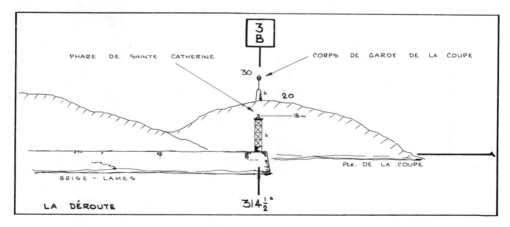

3B   the watch house beacon of la Coupe × St Catherine's light guides you clear to the south west of Chausée des Boeufs. It must be followed for 12 miles, so station a hand aft with the best pair of binoculars on board. Once past les Boeuftins 2·9m either continue along 3B, if you can still see the marks, or steer 135° (the currents in the bay of St Michel become progressively weaker). The next line

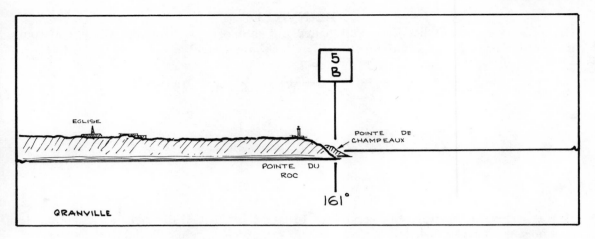

5B   Pointe de Champeaux × Pointe du Roc is likewise far off, 17 miles, but it safely leaves les Roches d'Agon *0·6m* a mile to port, la Cathue buoy (CE Clocher) ¾ mile to stb'd until Granville is reached.

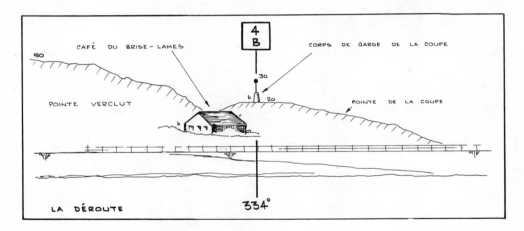

4B   the same watch house beacon of la Coupe × the right side of a house (café) at the root of St Catherine's breakwater is a similar departing mark from Jersey (Gorey). Five miles along the transit leave the Violet Channel buoy ('Jersey Violet' Mo 'V' B.27s) a few metres to stb'd, the two Anquette tourelles a mile to port. The mark can only be quit after 8 miles, i.e. when through the gateway of Plateau des Arconies *2·0m* and Frouquie Aubert *4·2m*, a gap only ¾ mile wide. From here to Granville there is nothing which isn't clearly buoyed.

In the corner, between Brittany and Normandy, harbours are few. Excluding Chausey, of which more later, Granville is the only one between Portbail (30 miles) and Cancale (14 miles). Perhaps this is unfair to Regneville but three miles of shifting, drying sand plus a moving channel marked by non-existent buoys doesn't appeal. Anyway, what harbour there is dries *8·5m*.

GRANVILLE

Granville is easy to find; like Carteret it shelters just south of a 50m headland. Coming in from the north, there are shallows and rocks well off the shore, chart B2.

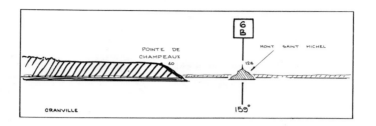

6B   clears to seaward of everything; Mont St Michel × the right of la Pointe de Champeaux. Don't be fooled by the fog signal of Pointe du Roc; while the lighthouse is perched on the cliff, 43m above the sea, the signal (Trompette 4 sons—60s) is on an insignificant tourelle (R) 300m to the north west. Keep the above mark 6B which leaves this tourelle, la Fourchie, 4 cables to port until

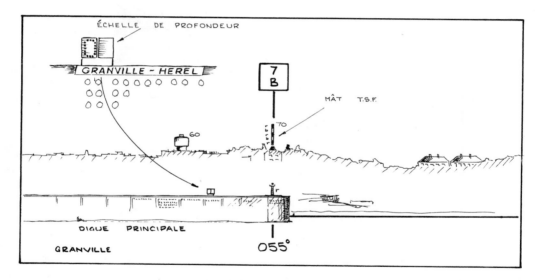

7B   a lattice radio mast × Hérel breakwater light, chart B3. This leaves le Loup tourelle (danger isolé Scint B) a cable to stb'd. None of the Granville lights is sectored but the pair of lights on the east and west jetties serve (Fixe V & R) to leave le Loup 60m to stb'd on a bearing of 013°.

Although the new Port de Plaisance de Hérel is for yachts, there seems no trouble in using the Port de Commerce for drying out alongside. Try the west jetty about the *6·3m* sounding, mud with a firm bottom. Or the Quai du Pan Coupé, firm sand. La Jettée Est is reserved for the Jersey and Chausey ferries. With the harbourmaster's blessing one can lock in to the Bassin á Flot. If the actual rock of Le Loup is awash, there is 2·0m as far as the gates.

56

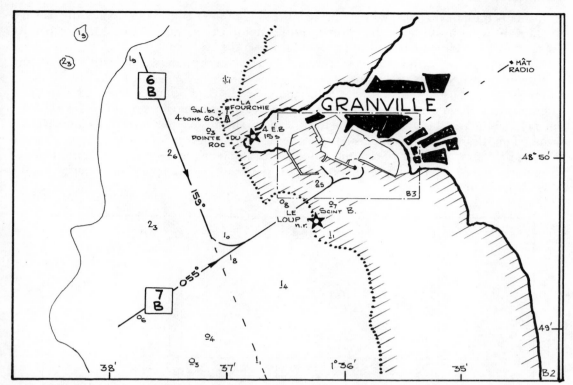

Chart B2—Entrée de Granville

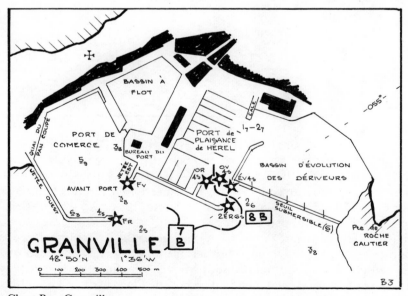

Chart B3—Granville

French Pilot I

Normally the gates are opened $1\frac{1}{2}$ hours before to 1 hour after High Water. Since the Bassin is for ships drawing up to 6·6m the cill details are unimportant. International signals control traffic. Priority is for commercial ships, then fishing craft, lastly yachts.

Now that the new marina (Hérel) is open with 800 berths, the best bet is to see if there is room among the special visitors' pontoons.

Chart B3 (p. 57) shows the route to enter and view 7B (p. 56) the tide level indicator. The automatic bascule gate is on view 8B. This clever device requires no human aid and works thus; when closed the gate holds water inside the marina to the all-over cill level of 6m above chart datum. This, the minimum level inside, gives between 1·7 and 2·7m of water, depending upon pontoon situation. There are two illuminated panels announcing, by day and night, depth of water for traffic. When the gate is closed the indicator reads 'o'. One panel faces out to sea, the other the pontoons inside.

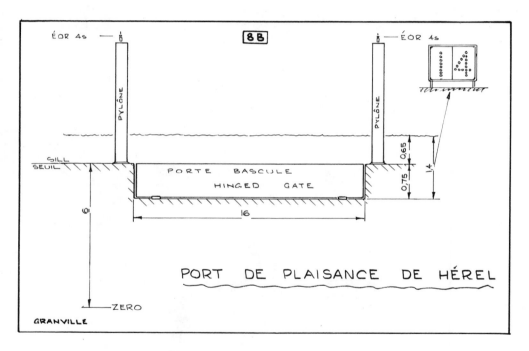

The tide rises, and when it has reached 6m is level with the all-over cill. The indicator still shows 'o'. As soon as the tide has risen a further 0·65m, the gate swings down and the indicator shows '1·4' i.e. the available depth to pass in or out. There is very little current at any time in the gateway in spite of the tide movement of up to a metre in 15 mins. The reverse operation happens on the ebb. The indicators continue to announce the depth—as much as 9m or so, for as long as the gate is in the dropped position.

Granville has all the facilities of a town of 15,000, and is the centre for a large region. Trains from Paris take $3\frac{1}{2}$ hours. There is a good bus service to Avranches where, in the 6th century, Bishop Aubert caused work to start on Mont St Michel. The fine museum displays documents and plans (planning permission even then?). The Port de Plaisance has a travel-hoist of 15 tons, a drying grid, a slip, showers, etc.

ILES CHAUSEY

From Granville, it is only 9 miles to the main anchorage in Chausey, an intriguing archipelago of islands, pools, bays and secure anchorages covering 15 square miles. It is clean all round the edges and beautifully marked. On Grande Ile live a handful of characterful romantics, torn as always, between the two choices open to small islands; the rattle of the till from visitors and the quiet of non-development.

Chart B4 (p. 60) contains the archipelago; chart B5 (p. 63) shows the main anchorage, the Sound. The other important anchorage is les Roquettes á l'Homme, about in the centre. Five channels serve the Sound, five end up at les Roquettes, two more are traverses, thus:

       1—Sound de Chausey from south
       2—Sound from passage à l'Est des Épiettes
       3—Sound from Grande Entrée, west side
       4—Sound from Grande Entrée, east side
       5—Sound from Passe de NW
       6—Roquettes à l'Homme from la Petite Entrée
       7—Roquettes from Passe de la Conchée
       8—Chenal des Roquettes à l'Homme
       9—Roquettes from Passe à l'ouest de l'État
      10—Roquettes from Passe Orientale de l'État
      11—Traverse, Chenal de la Rairie
      12—Traverse, Roquettes to Chenal de la Rairie

The east of Iles Chausey is better marked than the west, and

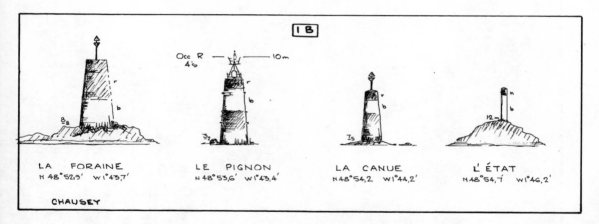

1B

LA   FORAINE
N 48°52,9' W 1°43,7'

LE PIGNON
N 48°53,6' W 1°43,4'

LA CANUE
N 48°54,2 W 1°44,2'

L'ÉTAT
N 48°54,7 W 1°46,2'

CHAUSEY

1B   pictures the four leading tourelles. Note that on chart B4 (p. 60) the 3m contour has been omitted; it is of no value and also too complicated.

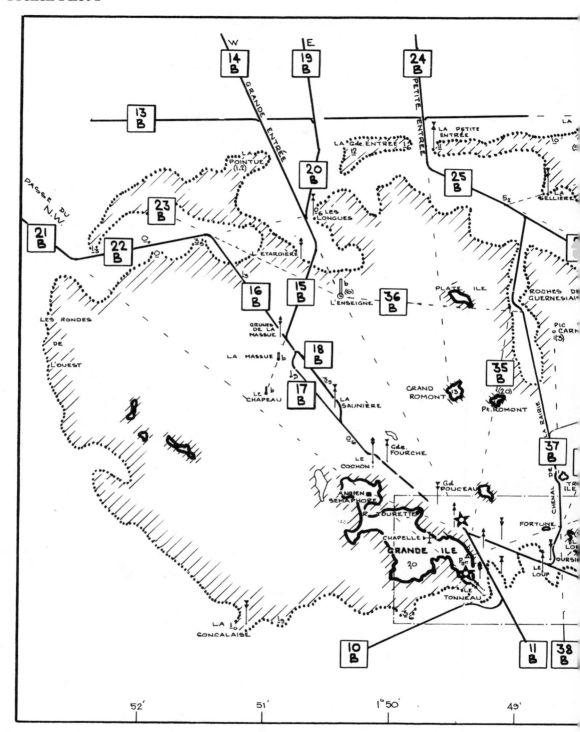

L'ÉTAT

PASSE DE L'OUEST DE L'ÉTAT

PASSE DE ORIENTALE DE L'ÉTAT

32 B

33 B

1 B

34 B

CANIARD DU SUD

LA CANUE

7s   1 B

48° 54'

55'

LE PIGNON

1 B
Occ R 4s

Pte MAUVAISE

LA MAUVAISE

LA CULASSIÈRE (4.4)

ROQUETTES À L'HOMME

41 B

L'HERBIER

53'

LE FORAIN

1 B

31 B

TOMIN

28 B

NERET

R.ANGO

ILES DES HUGUENANS

LA CONCHÉE

PASSE DE LA CONCHÉE

LIGNES DE NIVEAU
3m OMISE

TOURNIOURE

52'

3m CONTOUR OMITTED

FIS-COUS

OUEST DES

12 B

30 B

29 B

ILES CHAUSEY

47'   46'   45'   44'

B4

1—Sound de Chausey from south (1·0m)

Since the main centre of civilisation lies between the lighthouse and the church, the Sound is the obvious place to make for first; it has also the easiest and shortest entry. To clear the Roches de Bretagne *3·6m* and other rocks line

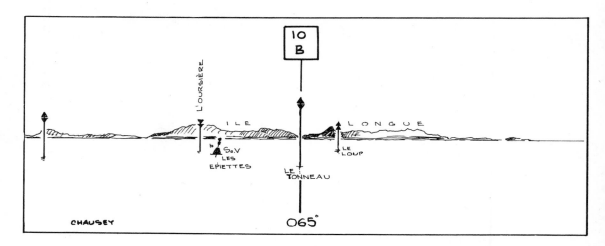

10B   the gap in Ile Longue × le Tonneau balise (CE) but when a cable from the balise steer east so as to leave the balise 100m to port and join

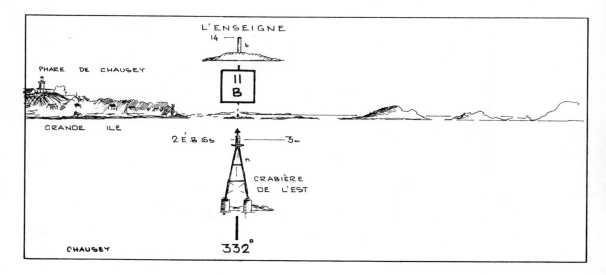

11B   the main mark for the Sound, l'Enseigne tourelle × Crabière de l'Est, a framework light structure. This transit leaves les Épiettes lit buoy 50m to stb'd. If you want to play safe, there is another metre of water if, when abreast of the lighthouse, you borrow 25–30m to the east for a cable's length. But even at MLWS there is 1·4m over this patch which is sand.

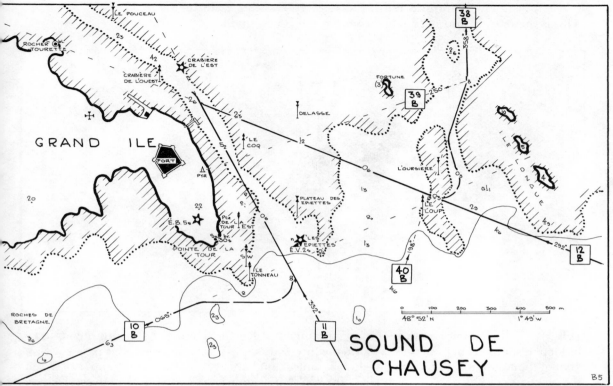

Chart B5—Sound de Chausey

Leaving Crabière de l'Est 50m to stb'd, you now enter the anchorage where there are plenty of mooring buoys between here and le Pouceau balise (CS). Granville Yacht Club have laid about a dozen.

This is the only night entry possible, and line 11B takes you into the centre of the 6° white sector of Crabière de l'Est light.

Landing can be made at the main slip, north of the fort—lying alongside is forbidden—or at the low-water stage NE of the fort.

2—Sound from Passage à l'Est des Épiettes (*2·3m*)

This is the normal approach when coming in from Granville.

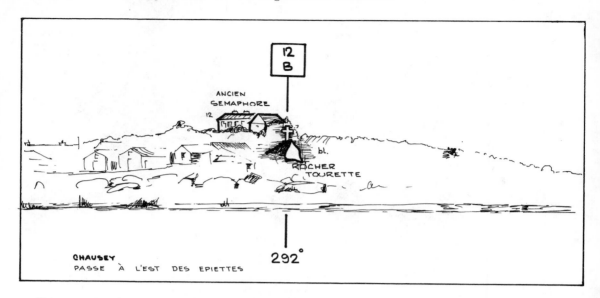

12B   the right hand side of the old semaphore × Rocher Tourette. The latter tends to be hidden in summer, but the rock is painted white and on top is a stone cross. This passes within 30m of the south of Ile Longue, but there is almost 4m here. There is a *o·3m* sand bar between the two balises l'Oursière (CS) and le Loup (CN), and again a sand/mud neck between Delasse (CS) and le Coq (CN) before passing into the anchorage.

3—Sound from la Grande Entrée (west side) (*3·5m*)

There is a common clearance mark for this and the two following approaches which leaves all the dangers to the north. Line

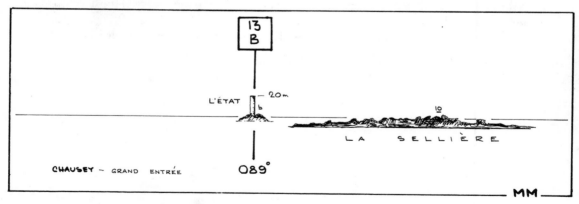

13B   tourelle de l'État × northernmost rocks of la Sellière. But the channel proper starts with an unmistakable man-made mark, this is

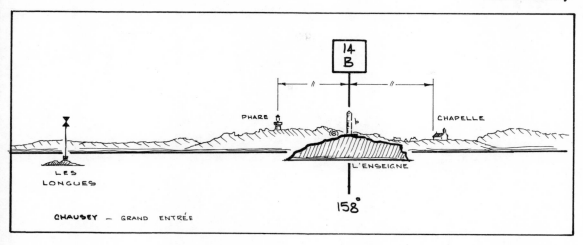

CHAUSEY — GRAND ENTRÉE

14B tourelle de l'Enseigne midway between the lighthouse and the chapelle. Almost the same transit, but the lighthouse × l'Enseigne (156°) is the traditional route from Jersey to Chausey. If followed northward it takes you immediately to the east of les Caux des Minquiers (NE Minquiers buoy). To continue, leave les Longues balise (CW) 50m to port and when $1\frac{1}{2}$ cables past, take

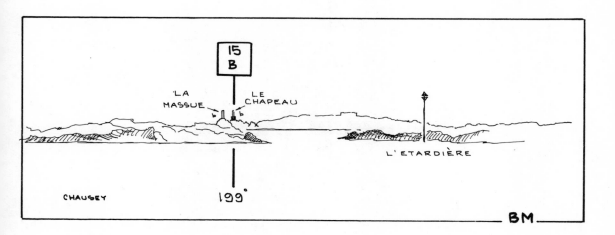

CHAUSEY

15B le Chapeau tourelle × la Massue tourelle (both white) for half a mile until, when about 50m from Grunes de la Massue balise (CE) (16B)

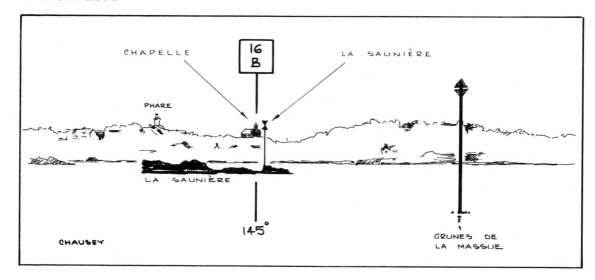

16B la Chapelle × la Saunière balise (CW). Immediately you are abreast of la Massue tourelle you must decide on one of two courses.

If above half tide (rise of 7·0m) take the channel passing SW of la Saunière. It passes over a sandbank *4·6m* but, with enough water, is safer than the alternative, later described.

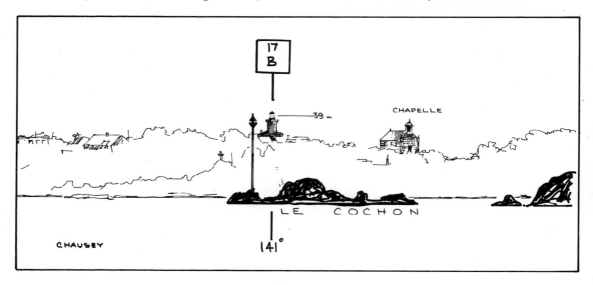

17B the lighthouse × le Cochon balise (CE) which leaves la Saunière balise about 15m to port. Follow this for $\frac{3}{4}$ mile until some 100m from le Cochon, make a dog-leg to the north east and pass midway between the gateway of le Cochon and la Grande Fourche balises, and so into the anchorage.

If, however, there isn't enough water for transit 17B, or the tide is below half ebb (7·0m rise) you must take the alternative route to the NE of la Saunière.

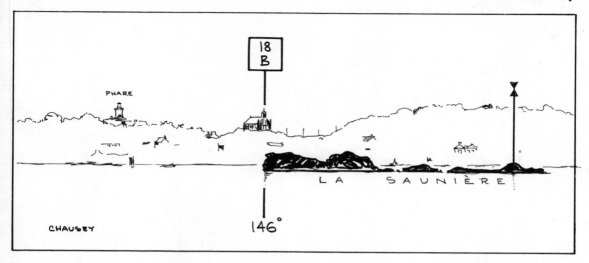

18B   the chapelle × the left face of la Saunière rock. This channel only dries *3·5m* but the reason why it isn't always used in preference to line 17B is that you are lost unless the top of la Saunière rock is showing. Turning to view 18B there is a ledge jutting out, but not shown, to the left of the east face. It is only half a metre wide and serves as a depth gauge for this channel; when it is awash there is 1·8m throughout. However, continuing along 18B, leave la Saunière rock 50m to stb'd, continue making a handrail so as to join

17B   (p. 66) 141°, and thus to the anchorage.

4—Sound from la Grande Entrée (east side) (*3·5m*)

This is almost the same as the previous channel, but instead starts further east. The French give it as a recommended alternative under sail.

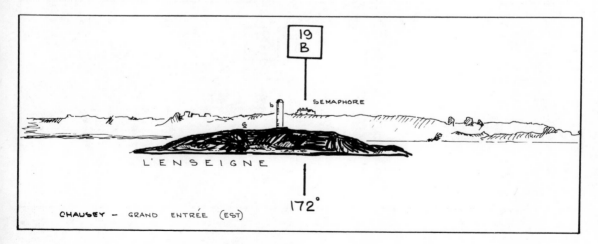

19B   the semaphore × l'Enseigne tourelle, until abreast of la Grande Entrée rock *12·0m* then alter course slightly to the westward (20B)

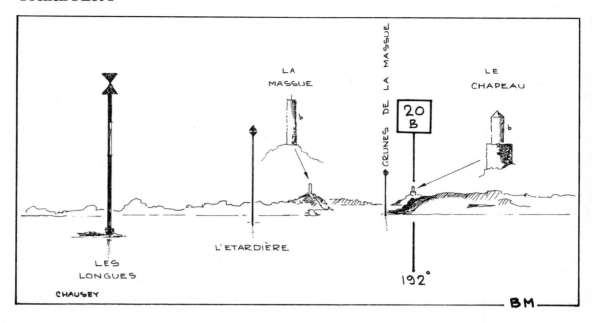

20B   le Chapeau tourelle × Grunes de la Massue balise (CE) to join
14B   158° (p. 65) and continue as before.

5—Sound from Passe de Nord Ouest (*3·5m*)

Here is the recognised and only approach from the west

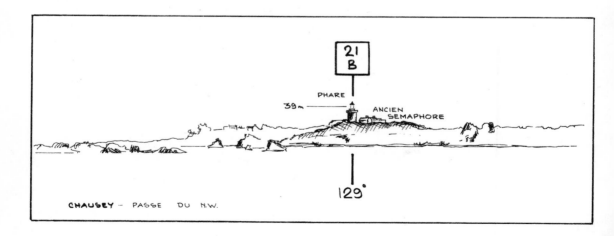

21B   lighthouse × semaphore, but stand by for a port turn on the edge of the graveyard, an easy man-made mark,

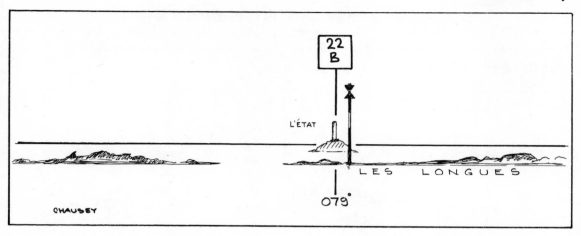

22B tourelle de l'État × les Longues balise (CW) and keep the objects as shown and don't turn to stb'd too soon for the next mark since you must leave, only 15m to stb'd, a head drying *3·5m* and to make sure of this critical elbow here is a breast mark,

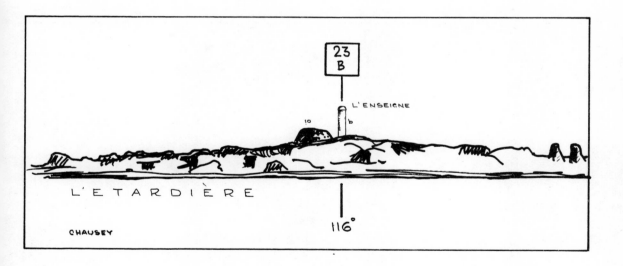

23B l'Enseigne tourelle × the summit of l'Etardière, 10m high, an unmistakeable rock. The next mark takes over now,

16B The chapelle × la Saunière balise, 145° (p. 66) and so on to the anchorage.

6—Roquettes à l'Homme from la Petite Entrée (5·2m)

About in the centre of the whole boneyard there is a deep anchorage much used by sheltering fishermen and visiting yachts unable to face up to the pace and bustle of Grande Ile. The first entrance marks are,

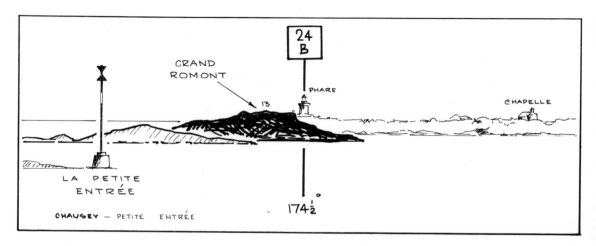

24B   the lighthouse × the west face of Grand Romont, 13m high. As a check, locate la Petite Entrée balise (CW) which has to be left about 50m to port. When only a cable past this balise look for the main Roquette channel,

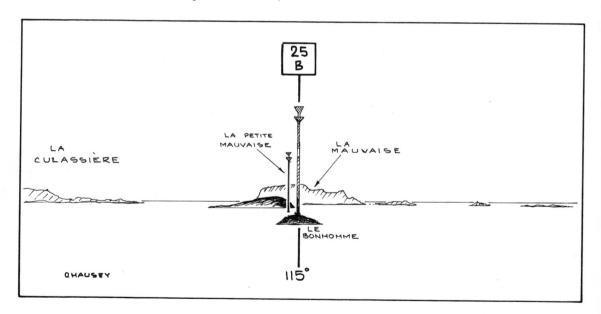

25B   Petite Mauvaise and le Bonnehomme balises (both CS) in line. Four cables along this line, look ENE for a breast mark telling of a slight change of course to stb'd,

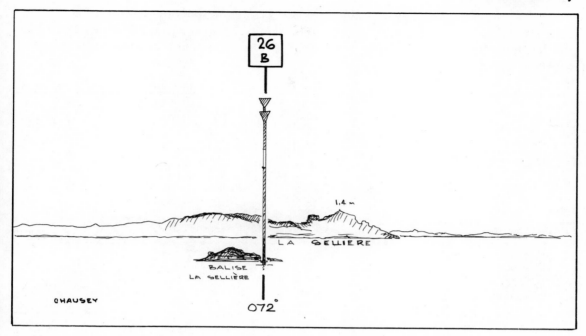

26B   la Sellière rock × the balise of the same name (CS) and then

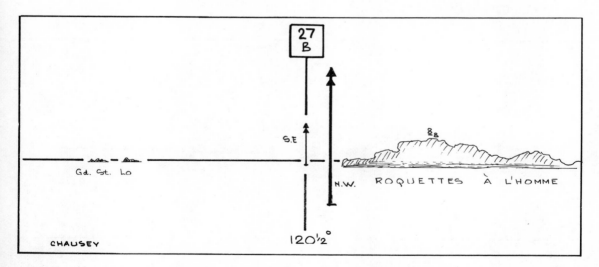

27B   the SE balise of les Roquettes à l'Homme × the NW one of the same name (both CN) which will serve for another mile fetching up at the actual anchorage of les Roquettes. You will see from chart B4 (p. 60) that there is a vast anchorage area, the maximum current is 2 knots at springs, 1 at neaps. This runs 9 hours to the NW starting 5 hours before HW St Malo, and 3 hours to the SE. The tides in the Sound are half as fast.

7—Roquettes from Passe de la Conchée (*0·3m*)

Here is the usual approach from Granville or the east but there are two rocks which have been the downfall of several boats, Tomin *5·5m* and Basse de la Conchée *2·5m*. One transit clears to the south of both,

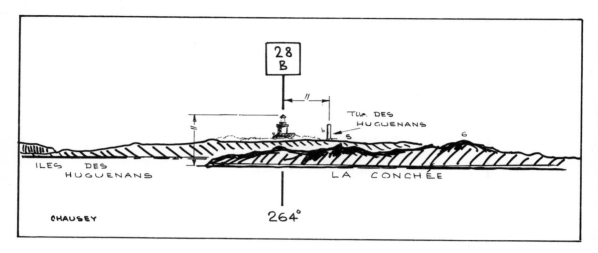

28B　　　the lighthouse open its height to the left of the tourelle des Huguenans. If going west, make a handrail a cable southabout from la Conchée 6m high, illustrated on view 28B and take the main channel marks

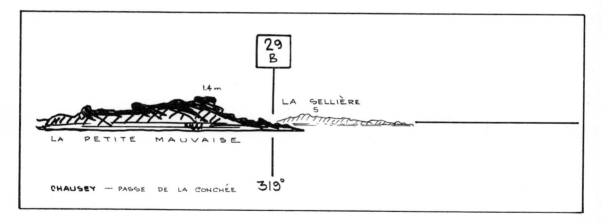

29B　　　la Sellière × the right side of la Mauvaise. From la Conchée this mark must be used for $1\frac{1}{4}$ miles until you can see through two gateways of balises. These are, continuing NW, midway between SE Roquettes (leave to port CN) and Mauvaise (leave to stb'd CS). There are no marks needed here but carry on through the second gateway, NW Roquettes (leave to port CN) and la Petite Mauvaise (leave to stb'd CS) until it is possible to use, as a stern mark, the two Roquettes balises, 27B (p. 71).

8—Chenal des Roquettes à l'Homme (7·0m)

This is the deepest channel in the Iles de Chausey and leads to the Beauchamp anchorage. This isn't marked on chart B4 (p. 60), but is where I've put the 31B square. The recognition marks are

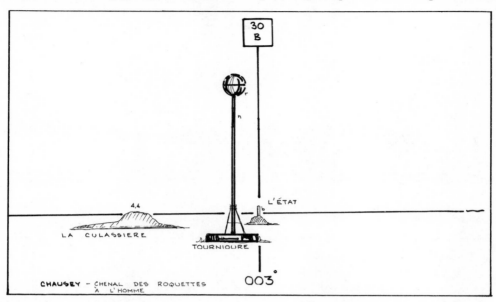

30B   tourelle de l'État × le Tournioure balise. Tournioure, (danger isolé) is a mid-channel balise and can be passed either side, though the west is steeper. Leave it 10m to stb'd and pick up

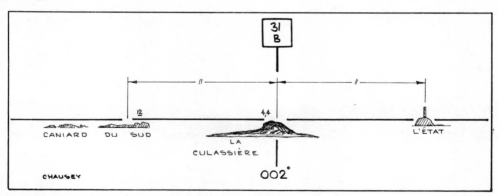

31B   la Culassière midway between Caniard du Sud and l'État. This rock la Culassière 4·4m high, has magical qualities, it looks like a modern sailing hull inverted, in this view rudder to the left. But it appears the same way from wherever it is seen. One of the Chausey pilots dismissed the phenomenon with a shrug 'Mais voilà, il bouge'.

Mouillage de Beauchamp is some half mile north to south along line 31B, depths between 8m and 12m, current as at les Roquettes à l'Homme anchorage. The same line may be followed north to join 29B (see opposite).

73

9—Roquettes from Passe à l'Ouest de l'État (*1·9m*)

Coming from the north-east there are two channels of equal importance, ease and depth. The first is possibly quicker to locate, thus

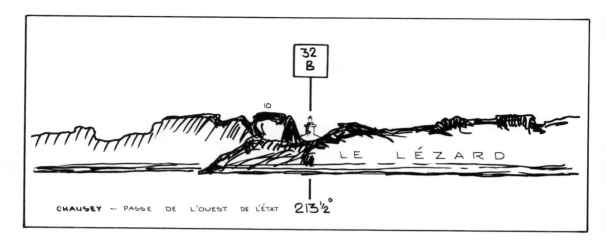

32B   the lighthouse × the notch in le Lézard, an unmistakeable rock 10m high, and this single mark takes you right in to the Roquettes anchorage.

10—Roquettes from Passe Orientale de l'État (*1·9m*)

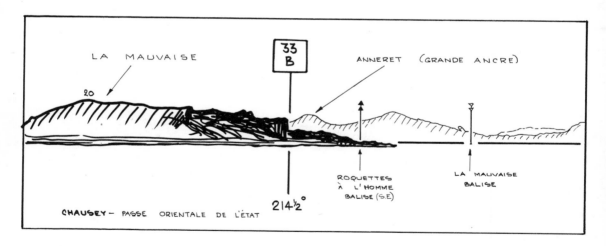

33B   The left hand hump of Anneret × the right face of la Mauvaise. Anneret is the correct and local name for Grande Ancre and in my sketch it is shown as one profile. Strictly the SE hump should be named Petit Anneret. Anyway, a couple of cables before reaching Mauvaise, alter course southward to take a stern mark,

74

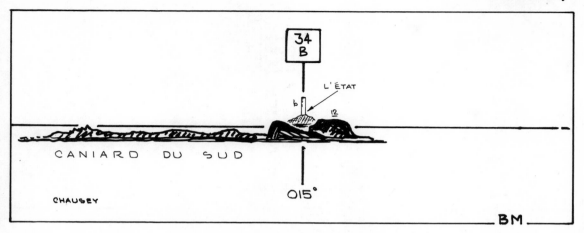

34B   l'État tourelle × the east heads of Caniard du Sud, which passes about midway between la Mauvaise and la Culassière and into the anchorage once again.

11—Traverse, Chenal de la Rairie (*1·om*)

This is a most interesting channel from north to south right down the middle of the maze of rocks. You will see when coming in from Jersey that there is deep water (5·2m) as far as the Roquettes via la Petite Entrée, whereas la Grande Entrée dries *3·5m*. This traverse therefore is used a lot so as to arrive in the Sound without a tedious battle of seven miles around the westward. There is never less than 3·4m of water at dead low water neaps and 0·5m at MLWS. You start just south of la Sellière balise and the first part of the channel when going southward is named Passe de Guernesiais. It changes name when abreast of Petit Romont to Chenal de la Rairie, the frontier being known fittingly as les Barrières.

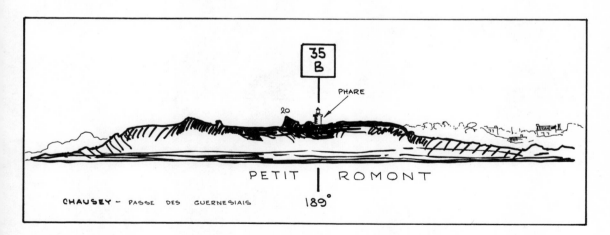

35B   the lighthouse × Petit Romont is the first mark, and when near Roches des Guernesiais make a 50m handrail to the westward. There is a convenient breast mark, (36B)

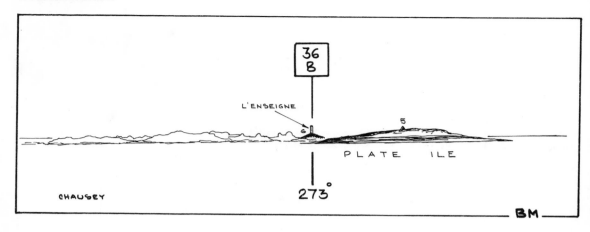

36B   l'Enseigne tourelle × the left slope of Plate Ile to aid in locating the next mark,

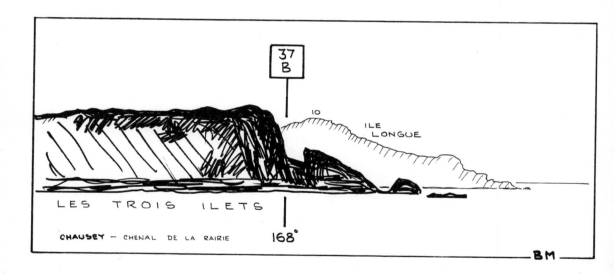

37B   the highest head of Ile Longue (10m high) × right side of les Trois Ilets. This mark lasts for almost a mile. When approaching les Trois Ilets, come to stb'd a few metres—they are steep to on their west side—and find a stern transit (see chart B5 on p. 63)

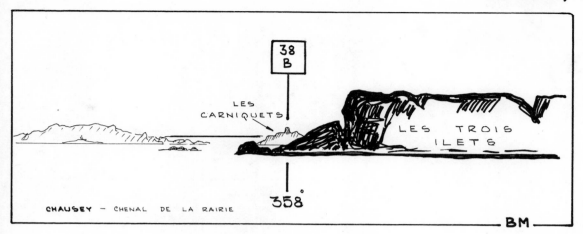

38B   Pic des Carniquets × the left slope of the same Trois Ilets. Follow this only for two cables until another breast mark shows up

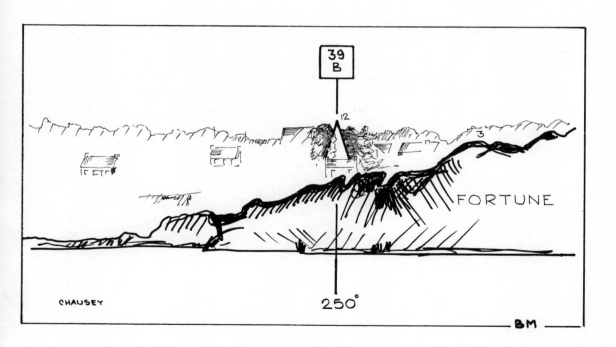

39B   a pyramid on Grande Ile seen to the south of Fortune, the clue to (40B)

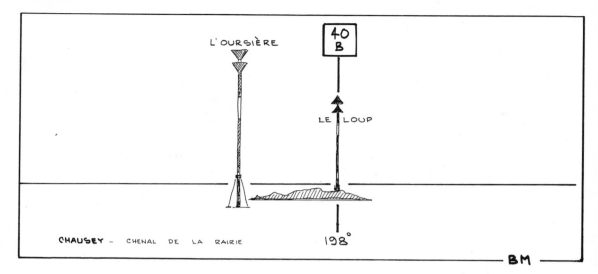

40B   le Loup balise (CN) opened to the right of l'Oursière balise (CS) by the amount shown. All you have to do now is to leave the nearest balise, l'Oursière 20m to stb'd and pass between it and le Loup to find yourself on line

12B   292° (p. 64) and there you are. The whole channel is less than two miles long and after all, if you aren't interested in a bit of intricate pilotage you wouldn't be reading this anyway! Now let's moor up and take your tattered nerves along to the hotel bar for a restorative.

12—Traverse, Roquettes to Chenal de la Rairie (*2·6m*)

There's only one more short cut through the middle of the forest and it connects the channel we have just come down with the anchorage by la Mauvaise. Going westward

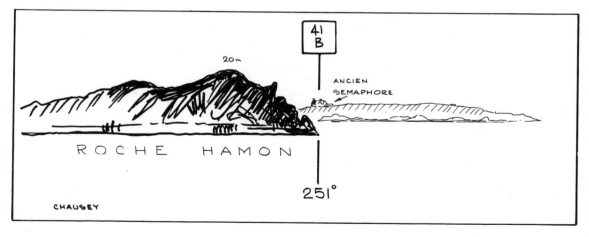

41B   the semaphore × the steep north face of the giant Roche Hamon, 20m high. Make a small handrail to the north, about 15m to pick up a stern mark

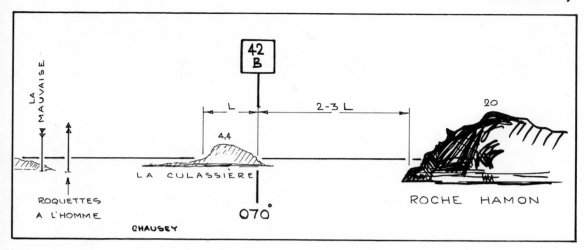

42B   that magic rock, la Culassière × two to three widths to the left of the same Roche Hamon. Keep it just so for half a mile until

37B   168° Chenal de la Rairie (p. 76).

    With luck Chausey will retain its charm for some time, since Grande Ile is mostly privately owned. The State governs a small area round the lighthouse only. M. Marin-Marie, the famous maritime painter and ocean traveller has his studio here.

    The pyramid in line 39B is no longer of navigational significance. It is the southernmost of a pair whose alignment (about 317°) divides the old-time fishing limits agreed between the men from Granville and those from Cancale. The imaginary line if produced, runs through Mont St Michel precisely, i.e. it divides Normandy from Brittany. The northern pyramid is today still functional; it's part of the hotel kitchen and the chef hangs his omelette pans on it.

    Perhaps the view that Chausey takes of the rest of the world is best summed up by their recently installed public telephone box. Within a few weeks M. le Curé started to grow ivy over its stark modernity.

PORT MER

Equidistant from Chausey and Granville is Pointe du Grouin the northern tip of a three mile stretch of coast. It is well worth a visit for we shan't meet a similar until inside the Rade de Brest; completely sheltered from the west, high cliffs covered in trees with vegetation down to a metre or so off the high water mark. The lighthouse marking the NE end of the reef off the point is la Pierre de Herpin in view

50B   What a dull time the watchmen must have in the semaphore in the same picture? They guard a cul-de-sac seldom used even by yachts. See chart B6 (p. 83).

Since no pilotage is required east of Pointe de Grouin how about starting about half a mile north of the semaphore? Sailing from here eastward there is a deep channel between the lighthouse Pierre de Herpin and the rock of the same name, called le Grand Ruet ¾ mile wide. Use the SW half for not only are there *3·6m* rocks a cable SW of the light, but a shoal of 1·1m about the middle.

A commonly used short cut is the next shoreward channel, le Petit Ruet just over a cable wide but 7m deep;

51B   Mont St Michel well open to the right of Roche Herpin. This mark is to avoid Basse des Pignonets o·1m, on the south side of this channel.

Although there is 6m in the channel between Ile des Landes and the Pointe du Grouin the tide runs hard and, by a curious fluke, nearly always northward. However, since our pilotage is aimed to finish up in Cancale we shall take it north to south. The northerly current reaches about 3 knots at about HW. St Malo, but after HW + 3 and before HW − 1 hour it isn't supposed to exceed half a knot. The Chenal de la Vieille Rivière has but one mark,

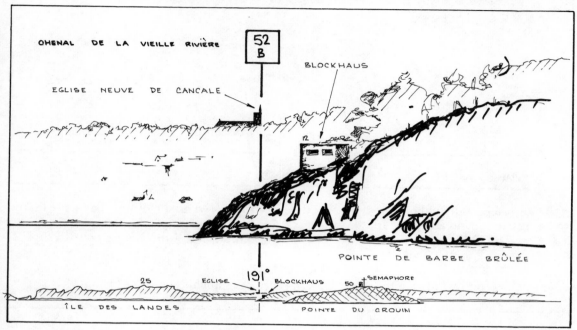

52B Cancale Church open to the left of a blockhaus on Pointe de Barbe Brûlée. Don't close it more than shown or it will be too close to the steep-to rocks below the semaphore. When abreast of the semaphore you may forget the transit and take the middle. At the foot of 52B is a far-away view which helps. Leave the blockhaus a cable to stb'd until,

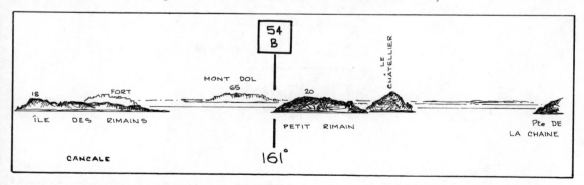

54B Mont Dol × the left side of Petit Rimain which will take you for over a mile down the coast. But there is a delightful anchorage right here before doing so, Port Mer.
  The entrance is straightforward, (53B)

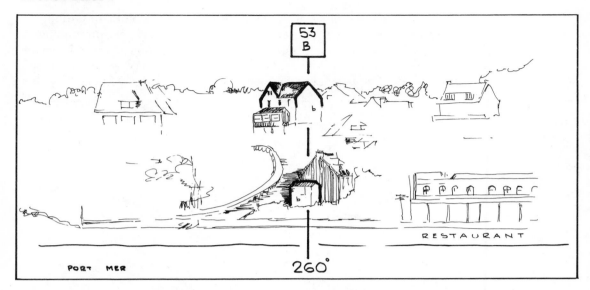

53B   a prominent house × a shed, both on the road down to the beach. There are many moorings here, sand and mud and this transit is merely to avoid some rocks, *5·4m* on the north side of the small bay. There is a village shop and restaurant but little else, except two slips.

PORT PICAIN

A few cables southward there is another, even more snug anchorage, Port Picain.

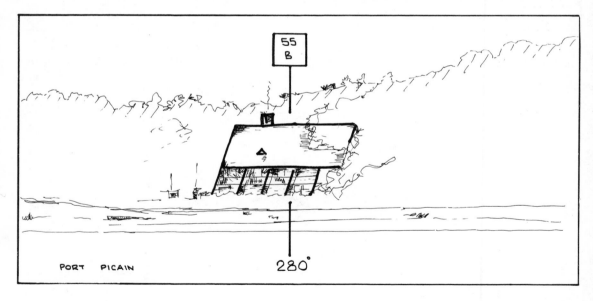

55B   which avoids rocks both sides, shows the picture of a modern architect's dream house at 280°. There is a slip, a tap nearby and a summer campsite.

82

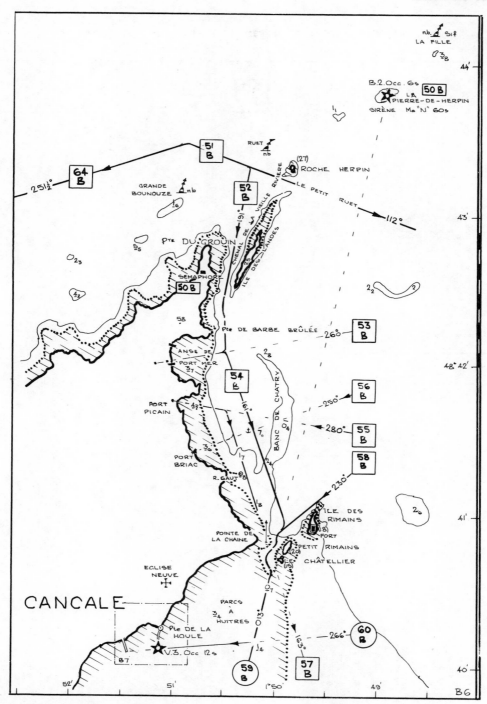

Chart B6—Rade de Cancale

PORT BRIAC

Right, so you don't like campers? Try Port Briac for seclusion.

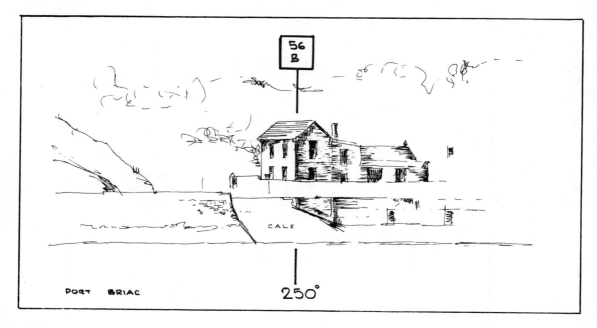

56B   the front of the only house visible × the only slip visible. Nothing else is visible
either.

CANCALE

If you are still bent on sailing down to Cancale, there is a danger to avoid, Rocher Gaut *0·8m* and to clear outside by some 50m use

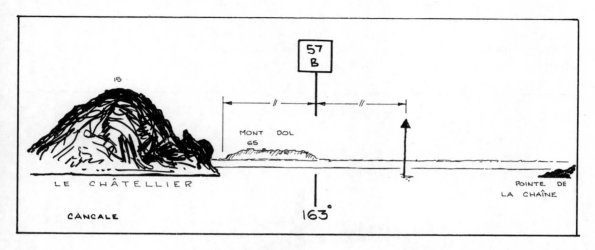

57B   Mont Dol its width to the left of the balise (stb'd) off Pointe de la Chaîne.

If there isn't enough water to carry on to Cancale here is the place to anchor, on line 54B and on the Port Briac marks 56B, in 7m mud and sand. The inshore approach to Cancale is just north of Ile des Rimains,

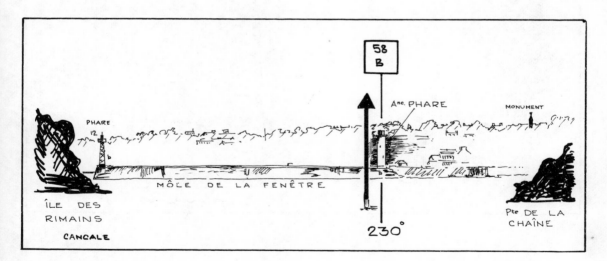

58B   the old lighthouse of Cancale × the balise of Pointe de la Chaîne. When within 2 cables of the balise take the mid channel between it and the 20m high Petit Rimains. As Cancale is the largest oyster port in Brittany, the beds are also large, but a simple mark leads to seaward.

85

59B   (no view) Pierre de Herpin lighthouse seen to the right of the gap you have just come through; Pointe de la Chaîne and le Châtellier. When the two breakwaters open out, line
60B   (no view) you are clear to the south of the precious bivalves (see chart B7).

Cancale is a charming fishing town where happily tourists rate lower than crustacés and coquillages; not that there aren't several good restaurants. There are chandlers and shops a-plenty, taps on the quays and a frequent bus service to St Malo. Drying berths abound but the southern half of the Môle de la Fenêtre is for fishing boats. The west side of the Epi de la Houle—which is the correct, old-time name of the port—seems little used.

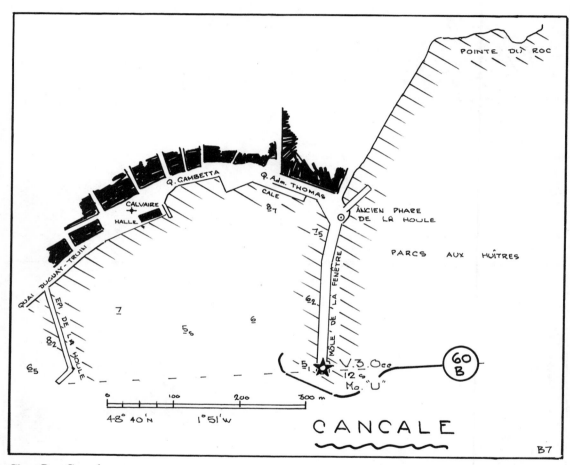

Chart B7—Cancale

ROTHÉNEUF

Between Pointe du Grouin and St Malo there are ten miles of rugged northwest facing coast with three or four rather temporary anchorages, where a few locals keep summer moorings. The inshore passages are deep, well defined and less boring than standing off the obligatory 2 miles. Six miles westward Rothéneuf will be our next harbour, so let's go back to about a half mile north of Pointe du Grouin and, while still on chart B6 (p. 83), take

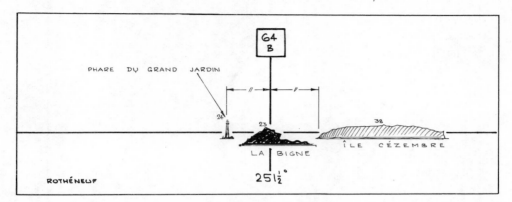

64B   la Bigne midway between Grand Jardin lighthouse and Ile Cézembre. Fair visibility is needed—the light is 10 miles away and one of the main St Malo marks.

We can now swap to chart B8 (p. 88) where you will see that this mark takes you inside the dangerous reef of les Tintiaux and north of les Cadins 7·7m. When abreast of les Tintiaux there is a small fair-weather anchorage to the south-east, Fort Duguesclin.

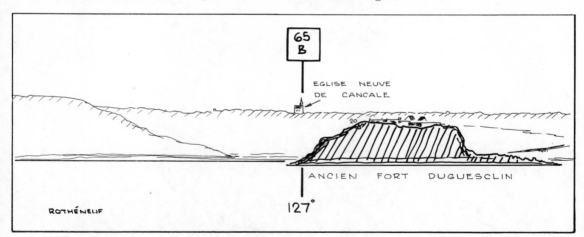

65B   Cancale Church × the left side of a 20m high island surmounted by an old fort. At a cable and a half from the guns, turn due south and find a space among the several boats moored there. It is a lonely spot on the lonely road from Cancale to St Malo. Bertrand du Guesclin harried the Brits until he died in 1380 and his fort is a private house with mainland access only at low water.

87

88

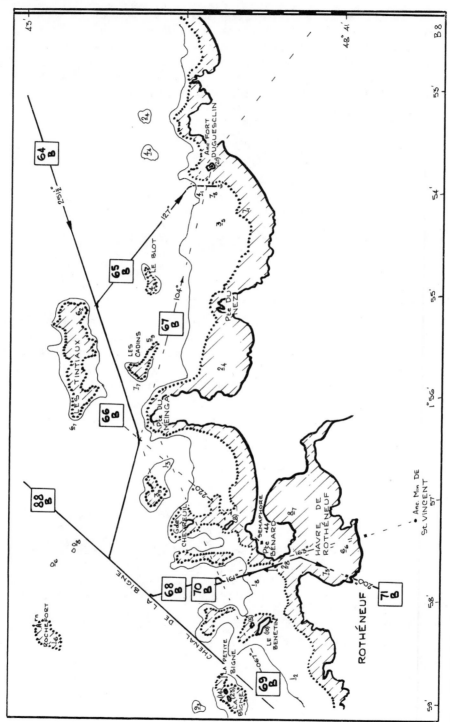

The current inside les Tintiaux starts running westward at HW St Malo, 2·7 knots max at springs; and starts to the east at LW max 2·5 knots. Neap rates are half these.

Continuing along line 64B, look for a useful breast mark when a cable west of Pointe de Meinga,

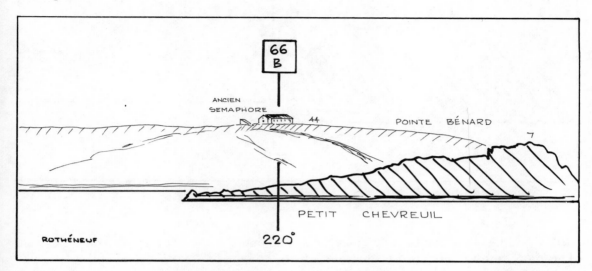

66B   Rothéneuf old semaphore × the extreme left side of Petit Chevreuil. The semaphore is now a private house and here is a stb'd turn on a stern mark

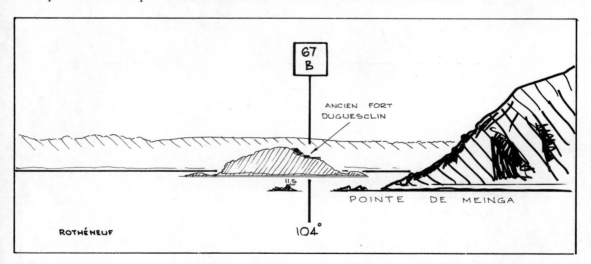

67B   Fort Duguesclin × the left of Pointe de Meinga. After a short ¾ mile you will be on one of the eastern transits for St Malo, Chenal de la Bigne. The mark is shown on p. 101 but the objects are the right hand part of Grande Bey × la Crolante white tourelle, line 88B.

Before St Malo comes Rothéneuf and four cables from where we joined the Bigne Channel here is the first entrance mark (68B)

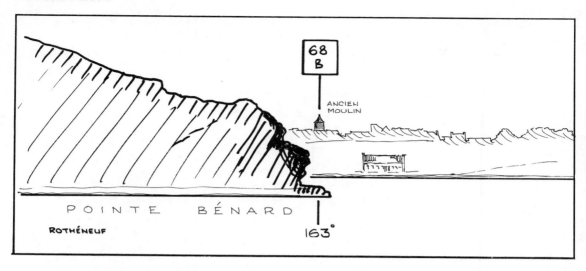

68B   the old windmill of St Vincent (now a house) × the right face of Pointe Bénard. This transit must not be used further north than the Bigne Channel marks, as there are too many troubles around Rochefort tourelle.

    The Rothéneuf entrance mark, 68B, after half a mile, moves to the west slightly when a breast mark arrives,

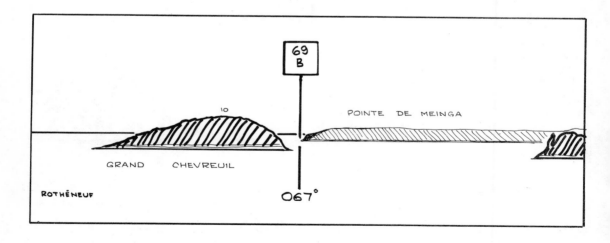

69B   Pointe de Meinga × the right of Grand Chevreuil about 10m high. When so, take

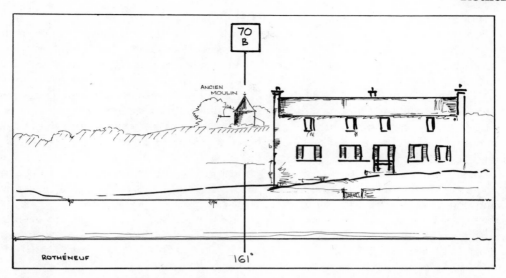

70B   that old windmill × the left gable of a large house on the beach in Rothéneuf. This line takes you between a stb'd balise and the rocks beneath the semaphore, into the enclosed Havre de Rothéneuf. The entrance dries *2·8m* and is about 75m wide, and after 2 cables past the balise head towards the yacht moorings clustered about the SW part.

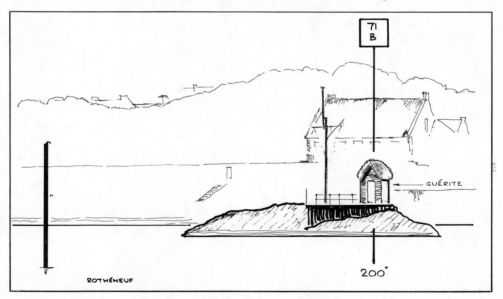

71B   Is a useful though not a vital mark, a large house × a charming thatched guérite (sentry hut) on a stone platform. The bottom of most of the west half of the harbour is level, hard sand and there are two slips and a 400m stroll to the village of Rothéneuf. Here are shops, restaurants and a garage—a pleasant backwater for a day or so, and only 20 minutes by frequent bus to St Malo.

ST MALO

City of corsaires, of discoverers, of statesmen, St Malo has thrust itself up from total destruction in 1944 to a fine city of some 45,000 inhabitants. Any town of that size which rebuilds itself in the architecture of the 16th century is worth a visit; how easy it would have been to have manufactured just another concrete Disneyland. The importance of sea trade over the centuries is shown by the towers and forts in the six-mile wide estuary, and the reason for the many marked channels was to suit sailing ships unable to tack readily.

The tides among the various channels are complicated though never greater than 2·4 knots at springs, and half that at neaps. I'm going, therefore, to quote the worst case in terms of rate, in Chenal de la Petite Porte, close to le Buron light (N 48°39.2′—W 2°03.4′). Here it is slack at HW (St Malo) when it starts to run toward le Grand Jardin light until the slack at LW when it starts to go St Malo-wards. The maximum speed is 2·4 knots at springs, 1·2 at neaps, which peaks happen 4 hours after and 3 hours before HW.

Of the seven channels, only the first two described can be used at night and all are on chart B9. Chart B10 (p. 107) shows the Rade de St Malo, termination of all the channels, and the entrance to the Port de Plaisance and St Malo locks. Chart B17 (p. 123) is the anchorage south of Ile de Cézembre and B14 (p. 115) and B15 (p. 119) cover la Rance.

1—Chenal de la Petite Porte, day and night
2—Chenal de la Grande Porte, day and night
3—Chenal du Décollé
4—Passage à terre de Nerput
5—Chenal de la Bigne
6—Chenal de la Grande Conchée
7—Chenal des Petits Pointus
8—Traverse, Chenaux de la Bigne à la Petite Porte
9—St Malo
10—St Lunaire
11—Dinard
12—St Servan
13—Ile de Cézembre
14—la Rance

Chart B9—Baie de St Malo

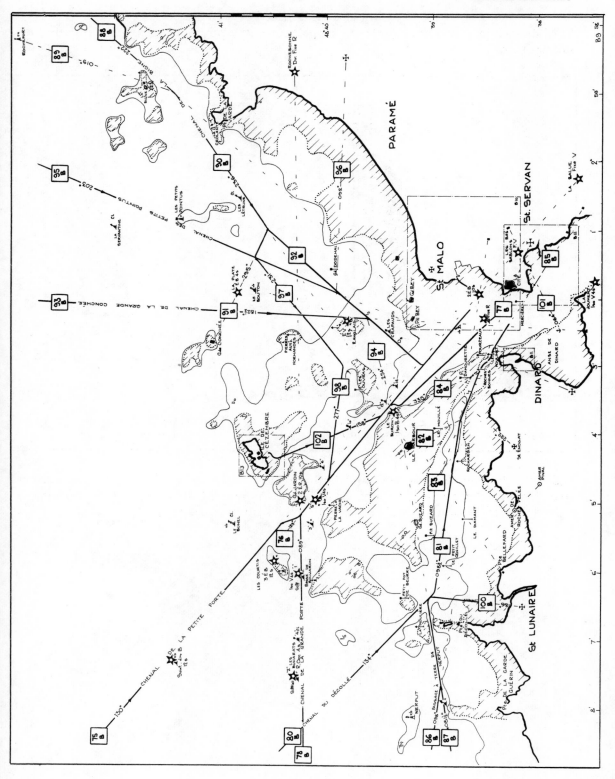

1—Chenal de la Petite Porte (8·6m)

St Malo's leading, best lit and easiest channel. Since it hardly changes course it is perfect for sailing. By day,

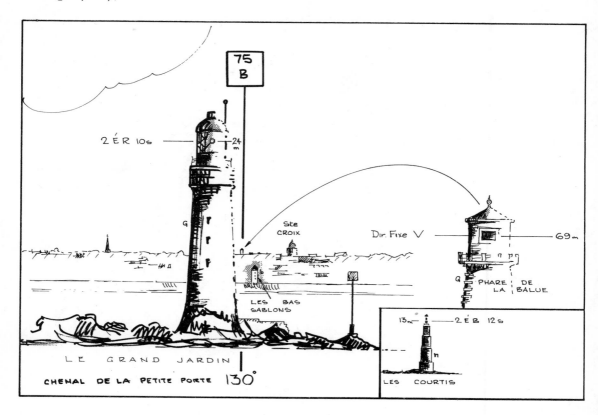

75B   la Balue light × le Grand Jardin light. The former only just peeps over various trees, blocks of flats and its granite shows up poorly. As soon as les Courtis—shown also on view 75B—is passed 1½ cables to stb'd steer south to pick up the final mark

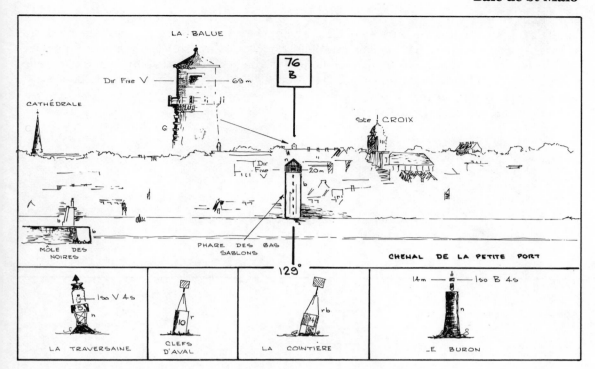

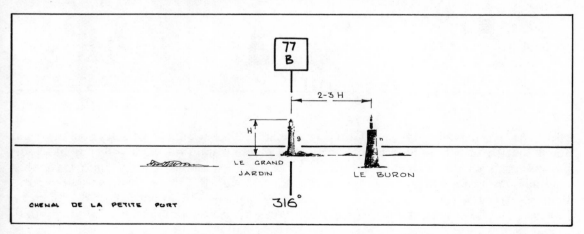

76B la Balue light again × Bas Sablons light, which takes you almost to the Môle des Noires. For the last mile, at cockpit height la Balue is lost to view. This isn't serious, because you will see on view 76B the Môle des Noires white light structure which can be used, when opened, as shown instead. If you are heading either to Dinard or up the River Rance there is no need to leave the Plateau de la Rance to stb'd. Instead pass to the south-west,

77B le Grand Jardin light 2–3 heights to the left of le Buron light. This is the clearance mark for Banc de Pourceaux incidentally. This whole channel starts at Basse de NE du Vieux

Banc buoy (not shown, N 48°43′ W 2°09′—CN cloche) to be left a cable to stb'd. Then leave a landfall buoy (Aterrissage, noire et blanche, Scint. Discontinu B. 12s) ½ cable to stb'd, les Courtis 1½ cables to stb'd, Banc de la Traversine (bouée '5' noire Iso.V 4s) 50m to stb'd, bouée '8' (rouge) a cable to port, les Clefs d'Aval (bouée '10' rouge) 1½ cables to port, le Buron tourelle ½ cables to stb'd, Basse du Buron (bouée '12' rouge) ½ cable to port, la Cointière (bouée '14' damier rouge blanc) a cable to port.

By night the same marks are used. Grand Jardin is a 15 mile light.

2—Chenal de la Grande Porte (5·8m)

The second important approach is from the west,

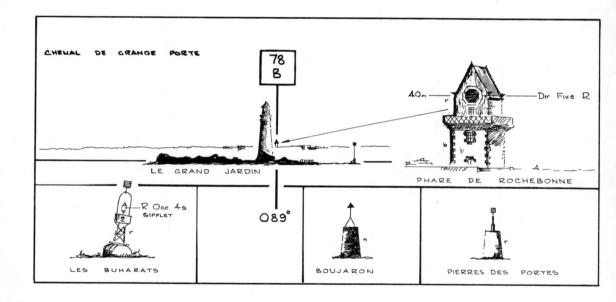

78B   Rochebonne light × le Grand Jardin light. The back mark is 4 miles from the front and is buried in a housing estate. Perhaps the magnification on view 78B matches your binoculars. Start at Banchenou (Bouée N 48°41′ W 2°11′—noire Fixe V) and leave this landfall buoy 4 cables to port, les Buharats (bouée '2' rouge, R. Occ. 4s—Sifflet) 50m to port, Bouée '4' (rouge clocher) 50m to port, Bouée '6' (rouge) a cable to port, Basse de Boujaron (bouée '1' noire Iso.V 4s—Sifflet) 25m to stb'd, Bouée '3' (noire) a cable to stb'd. Turn to stb'd to join

76B   (129°) Chenal de la Petite Porte (p. 95).

By night the same marks are used, Rochebonne has a 25 mile range, Grand Jardin 15.

Baie de St Malo

3—Chenal de Décollé (0·3m)

Though the above figure is the official pilotage depth the channel has silted slightly at the Dinard end—better take 0m as the least depth.

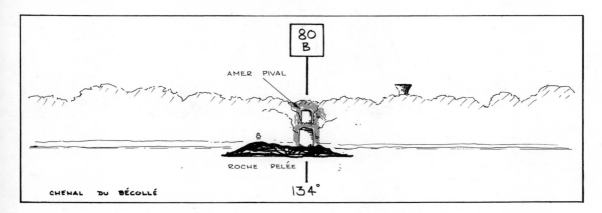

80B   Amer Pival × Amer de la Roche Pelée. These two small white towers would be fine, if someone like you and me sent the Ponts et Chausées a present of a saw, for the back mark is very nearly hidden in leafage. Note the position of a water-tower to the right of these marks. Keep exactly to the marks—there are rocks at the inner end only 30m on both sides. There is a 3 cable wide gateway, Petit Pot de Beurre (to port) and la Moulière (to stb'd) and when a couple of cables through, slow up and make dead sure of your position. Four transits more or less converge on this important crossroads.

     The first is the one you should still be on, the two amers 80B. Also here is St Lunaire entrance, 100B on p. 109. The third, 87B is dealt with on p. 100, and all these will serve to pick out the next marks.

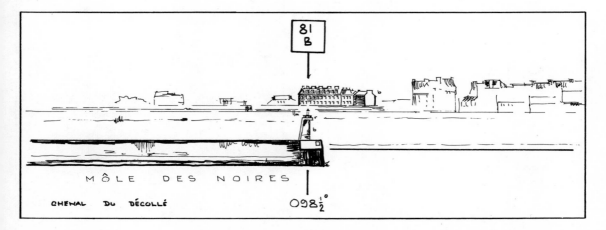

81B   the left side of a row of large houses in St Servan × Môle des Noires light. At the right end of these houses is a blank, white gable—most useful to help locate these houses. After 1¾ miles there is a breast mark to port,

97

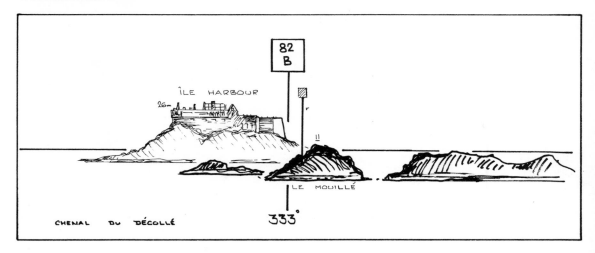

82B   right extremity of the Fort on Ile Harbour × le Mouillé balise. This marks the slight stb'd turn to

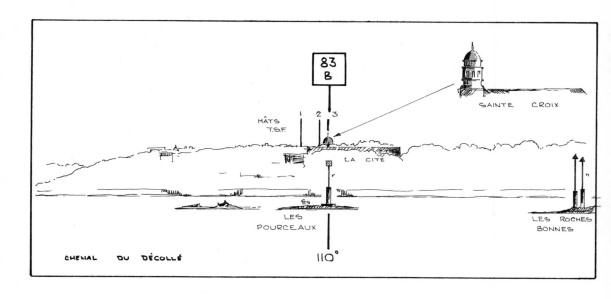

83B   There are three radio masts on top of the old Fort de la Cité; put Ste. Croix Church, St Servan, × the right hand mast and also × les Porceaux balise. Now here is where the channel has silted but if you take the following dog-leg from where I give you a breast mark

98

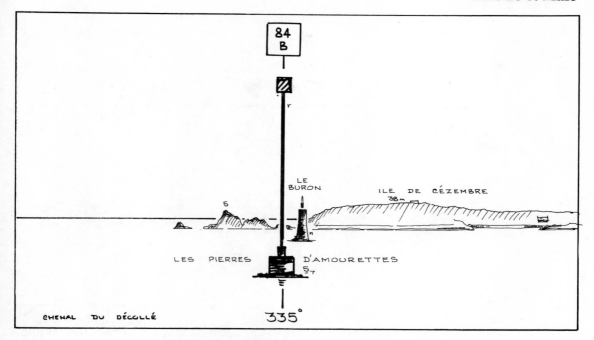

84B le Buron × les Pierres d'Amourettes balise, there is another metre of water. When past Roches Bonnes balise (50m to stb'd) head towards le Moulinet balise to avoid the build-up of sand to the south of Pourceaux. Leave Moulinet a mere 15m to stb'd and take line

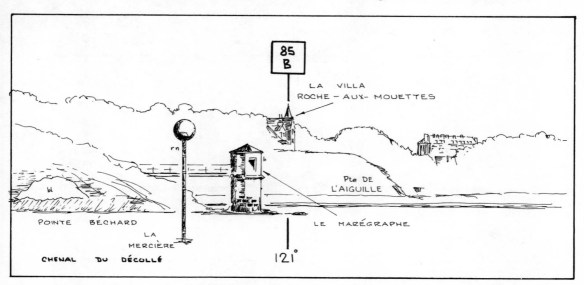

85B Villa Roche-Aux-Mouettes just to the right of the tidal gauge (marégraphe) exactly as shown. This leads out into the Rade de Dinard.

4—Passage à Terre de Nerput (0·3m)

This is a tributary to the Décollé just described. Its advantages are that it avoids searching the woodland for the Amer Pival and can be used as a popular route between St Malo and St Briac. There are twin approaches, the first a few metres north of Platier des Lardrières buoy, see chart B16 (p. 122).

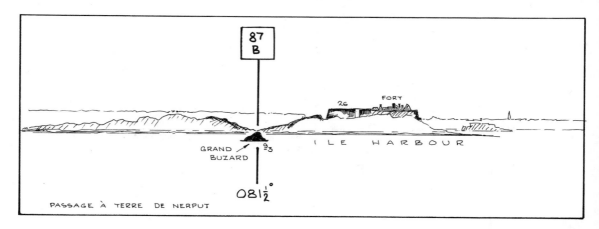

87B   the notch in the left side of Ile Harbour × le Grand Buzard, *9·3m*. This isolated rock is awash at MHW neaps and the marks take you through a 100m wide channel between la Moulière balise and the rocks north of Pointe du Décollé. There are 4m in this narrowest part. After 2 cables further on, rejoin

81B   (098½°) Chenal du Décollé (p. 97).

The alternative clears to the south of Nerput tourelle, chart B16 (p. 122), by a cable, and may be used for a seaward approach, say from Fort de la Latte.

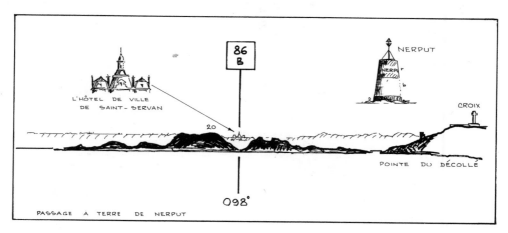

86B   Hôtel de Ville de St Servan × a notch in la Grande Roche du Décollé, which joins the previous alternative

87B   (081½°) the notch in Ile Harbour × Grand Buzard (see above).

5—Chenal de la Bigne (0·5m)

Here is the normal approach by the coastwise passage from Granville or equally well from seaward. First find yourself ¾ mile east of Rochefort tourelle (danger isolé)

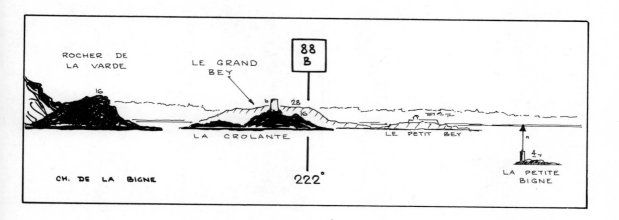

88B   the right part of Grand Bey × la Crolante tourelle. This leaves la Petite Bigne balise 75m to stb'd and la Bigne 23m high, 1½ cables to stb'd. When 3 cables past the balise check a port turn by a breast mark

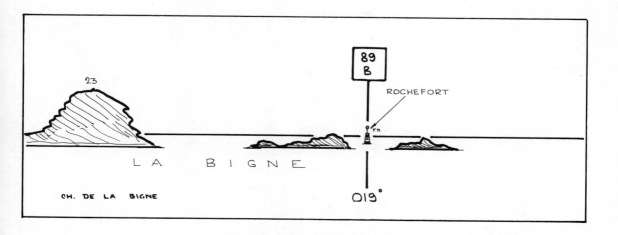

89B   Rochefort tourelle × la Petite Bigne rock. The next mark is not an easy one, which is why I give you a breast mark. It is 5½ miles distant.

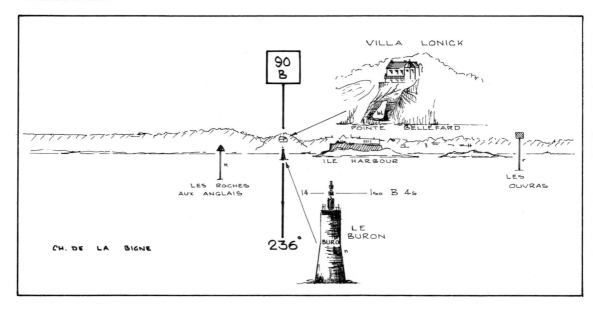

90B   Villa Lonick × le Buron tourelle. Villa Lonick is one of two fairly prominent houses above Pointe Bellefard, and a large rock at the base is painted white (blanchi). Follow this for $1\frac{1}{2}$ miles until a second breast mark arrives, very easy to find,

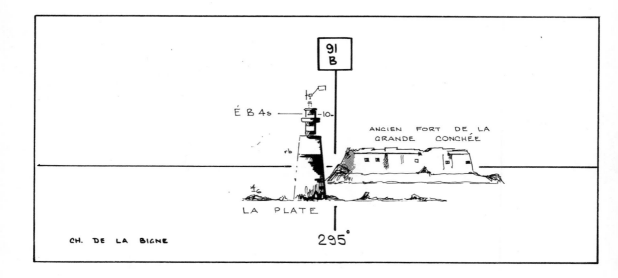

91B   the left face of the old fort on Grande Conchée × la Plate light, which has a wind-generator on top.

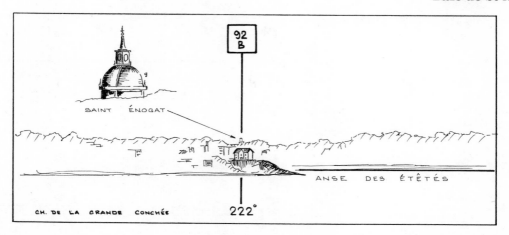

92B St Énogat Church × a house on the left of l'Anse des Étêtés. The pilot book calls this 'une maison remarquable' but today several millionaires and their architects have been let loose on this area. You have to use this mark for two miles so it is worth scanning the headland well; the house has a green roof, cream walls and no observable chimneys. The transit leaves Grand Dodehal balise 1½ cables to port, Roches Aux Anglais (bouée noire—É V 2s) a cable to stb'd, les Crapauds (bouée rouge) 50m to port. Half a mile later this channel joins
76B (129°) Chenal de la Petite Porte (p. 95).

6—Chenal de la Grande Conchée (0·5m)
This is frequently used by the hydrofoils from Jersey and the main mark isn't too difficult,

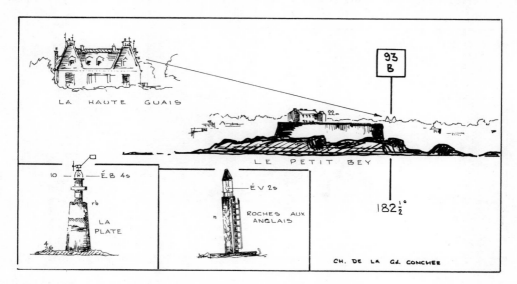

93B la Haute Guais × the right face of the Fort de Petit Bey. This leaves la Plate light 1½ cables to port, Pierres aux Normandes balise 2 cables to stb'd, Roches aux Anglais balise a cable

to stb'd and the lit buoy of the same name about 20m to stb'd, before immediately joining
92B   (222°) Chenal de la Bigne (p. 103). The breast mark for the junction is

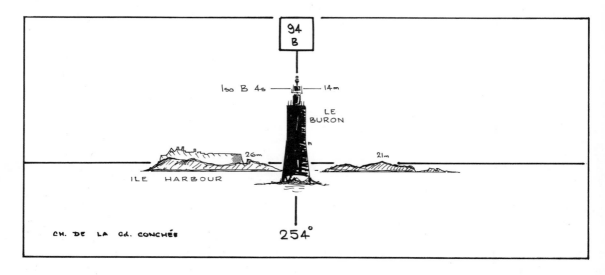

94B   the notch in the right part of Ile Harbour × le Buron light.

7—Chenal des Petits Pointus (0·5m)

Between la Bigne and la Grande Conchée channels lies this popular approach from 2½ cables east of la Servantine (bouée noire cloche).

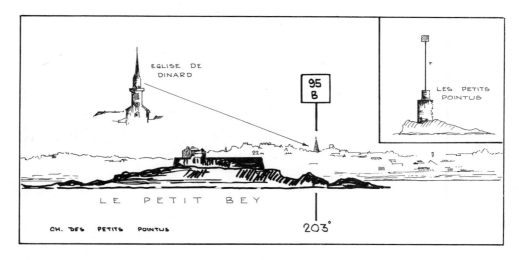

95B   Dinard Church open to the right of le Petit Bey Fort. On the same view is les Petits Pointus tourelle, leave it a bare cable to port and join, after 2 miles,
92B   (222°) Chenal de la Bigne (p. 103). The breast mark for the stb'd turn is

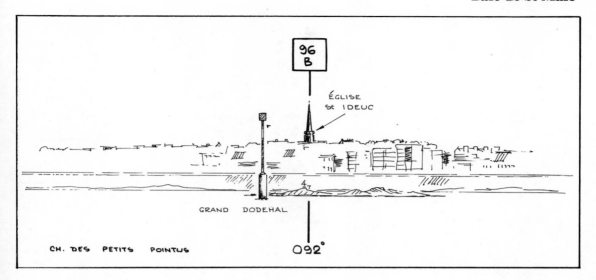

96B   St Ideuc Church × Grand Dodehal balise.

8—Traverse, la Bigne to Petite Porte (2·0m)

This short cut across various channels starts, sailing westward, from the Chenal de la Bigne 4 cables SW of les Létruns (bouée noire, cloche) and a former breast mark is a transit
91B   the left face of Grande Conchée Fort × la Plate Light (p. 102). Within 3 cables, going WNW, you cut across
95B   Chenal des Petits Pointus, (203°) and at the same time see line

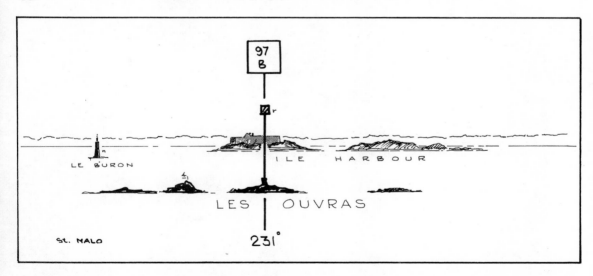

97B   the Fort on Ile Harbour × les Ouvras balise. 1½ miles later, after crossing the Chenal de la Grande Conchée, change to (98B)

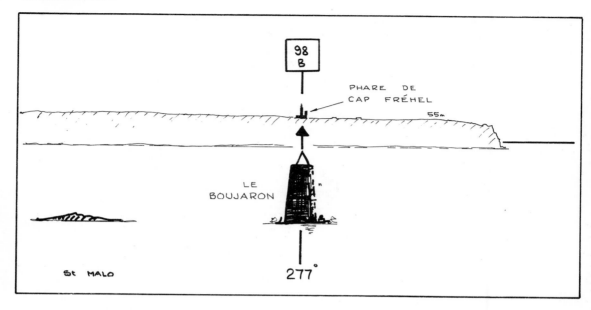

98B Cap Fréhel light (10 miles distant) × le Boujaron tourelle, which after a mile finishes up by joining
76B (129°) Chenal de la Petite Port (p. 95).

9—ST MALO

Since they are used to big ships in St Malo the entry is no problem. From the Rade de St Malo, chart B10, simply round the Môle des Noires and you are in the dredged channel aimed at the lock gates.

The Avant Port is the simplest. There is a one metre channel to two slips, just south of the Intra Muros or walled city. Fishing and ferry traffic is heavy.

The new Port de Plaisance des Bas Sablons keeps a number of berths for visitors. This marina has everything including an illuminated depth gauge on the north side telling the water over the *2·0m* drying fixed cill. Berths vary from 3m downwards. It is the best part of 3km walk to St Malo, so it is better to regard yourself as being in St Servan. St Malo, St Servan and Paramé have recently combined into one town. St Servan is a charming and ancient port, little touched by war damage and the centre is only 500m from the Bas Sablons marina. Here are restaurants, shops, a first class chandler, fuel, showers, etc.

The third and commonest choice is to lock in to the basins in St Malo. The lock is Écluse de Naye, size and location are on chart B10. The approach is on 072°, lit at night, (2 feux Fixe R) and the lock works normally from 2 hours before to 2 hours after high water. Depths inside vary between 6·6m and 7·3m.

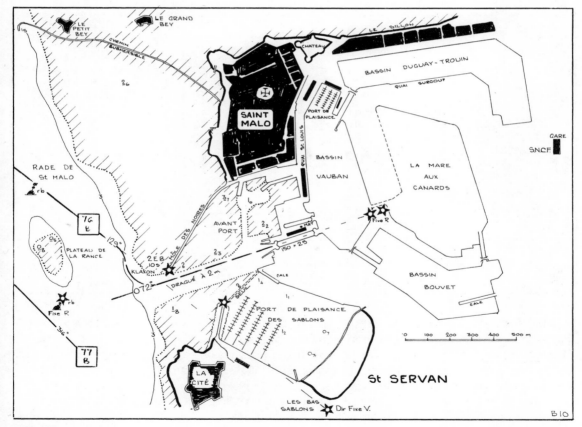

Chart B10—St Malo

French Pilot I

Vessel priority is: Commercial ships, sabliers, harbour craft, fishing boats and, very bottom, yachts.

Traffic signals for entry and exit are on a signal mast on the lockmaster's office on the north side of the lock. The mast has a yardarm with flags at both ends, plus a gaff with a flag. By night the yard has lights at the ends. The flags obviously show all round, but the lights are to be read when facing them. There are 12 signals in all but the six of interest to yachts are sketched below. Entry and exit are used in the sense into, or out of, the basin and not the lock. The flags used are plain red, plain green, International Code 'P'. A coloured list 'Signaux d'Entrée et de Sortie—Port de St Malo' is given free at the dockmaster's office. No answering signals need to be made from pleasure craft.

★ RED ROUGE	★ GREEN VERT	St MALO	"P"	★ BLANC WHITE
DAY – JOUR		OBJECT	NIGHT – NUIT	
		NO ENTRY DÉFENSE D'ENTRER	★	
		NO EXIT DÉFENSE DE SORTIR		★
		NO ENTRY OR EXIT DÉFENSE D'ENTRER OU SORTIR	★ ★	
		BOTH GATES OPEN BUT NO ENTRY 2 PORTES OUVERTES : DÉFENSE D'ENTRER	★	★
		BOTH GATES OPEN BUT NO EXIT 2 PORTES OUVERTES : DÉFENSE DE SORTIR	★	★
		BOTH GATES OPEN BUT NO MOVEMENTS 2 PORTES OUVERTES : DÉFENSE D'ENTRER OU SORTIR	★	★ ★

The Port de Plaisance is at the north end of the Bassin Vauban, though, with harbourmaster's permission, you may continue past a lifting bridge into the west end of the Bassin Duguay-Trouin. Both areas are within shouting distance of the showers, telephones, etc., where you can also wash your own clothes. St Malo, a town of 45,000 has every facility including sailmakers and repair yards.

Founded in the 6th century, by St Maclou from Wales, this fortified town has a raffish charm, legacy of her famous sons. Adventurers, pirates, privateersmen, statesmen, writers, whose pastimes brought the money to build and fortify their walled city.

10—ST LUNAIRE

Rather less fashionable than its victorian upstart neighbour Dinard, St Lunaire is a pleasant holiday centre with a sheltered sandy bay.

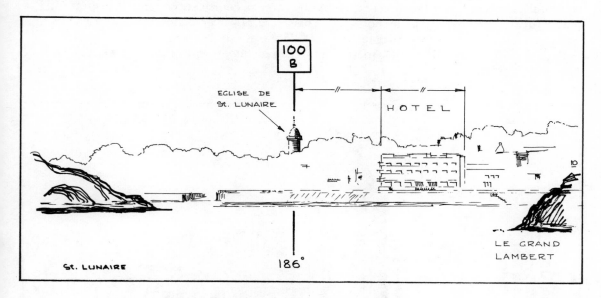

100B   The church open to the left of a gaunt hotel on the promenade is the entrance mark which leads to the east of Grand Lambert. The same mark was used for a breast mark for the Chenal du Décollé. There is a sandy estuary, south-east of the beach, drying about *8·5m* much used by boats in winter, with a road bridge at the head.

11—DINARD

In about 1840 some enterprising developer—reportedly American—must have had interesting thoughts while sipping his cognac in a small fishing village near the town of St Énogat. By the turn of the century Dinard was exclusively genteel and, of course, thoroughly British. It still has a lingering but vigorous air of 'le snobisme'. They have, however, a most hospitable yacht club. See chart B11. The new moorings for the Port Public are under construction.

Anse de Dinard dries from 3 to 4 metres, though many moorings are laid in a metre or two, on the river edge. Line

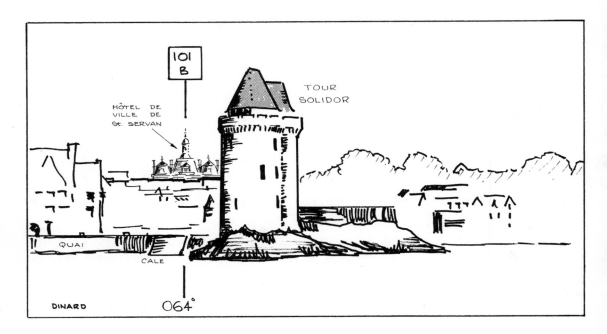

101B　　St Servan Hôtel de Ville × Tour Solidor is a useful line for anchoring. There is ample and secure drying almost anywhere.

At the northern end of the Anse there are drying berths *4·7m* alongside the quay in l'Anse du Bec de la Vallée. This, and the adjacent low water slip, are seldom used by ferries to St Malo since the hydro-electric barrage in the Rance was built.

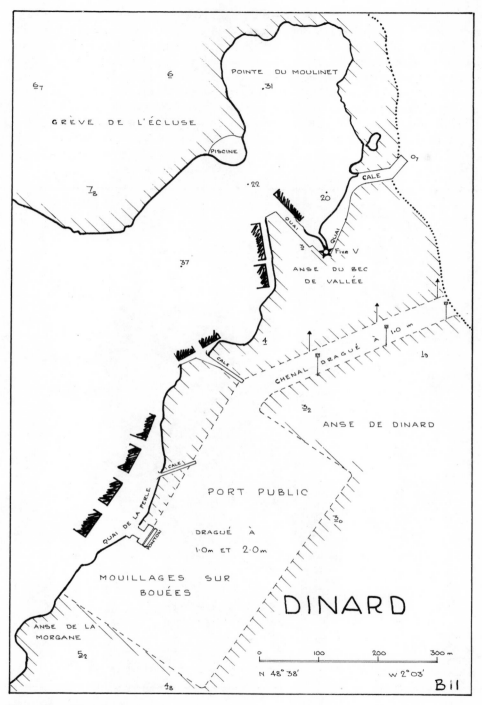

Chart Bɪɪ—Dinard

French Pilot I

12—ST SERVAN

The waterfront of this beautiful old town is dominated by the 12th century Tour Solidor. At one time a prison—British names are carved on the doors—today it is the Musée International du Long-Cours Cap Hornier. If you have sailed round that cape, you may join the distinguished society whose headquarters it is.

Excellent drying space can be found in l'Anse de Solidor, firm sand. On chart B12 where the words 'Tour Solidor' appear is the harbour proper, called Port St Père and is used by fishing boats. The NE side, drying *6·om* is out of their way for berthing alongside. Line 101B, on p. 110, is a most useful entrance transit as it clears to the NW of the Banc de Solidor.

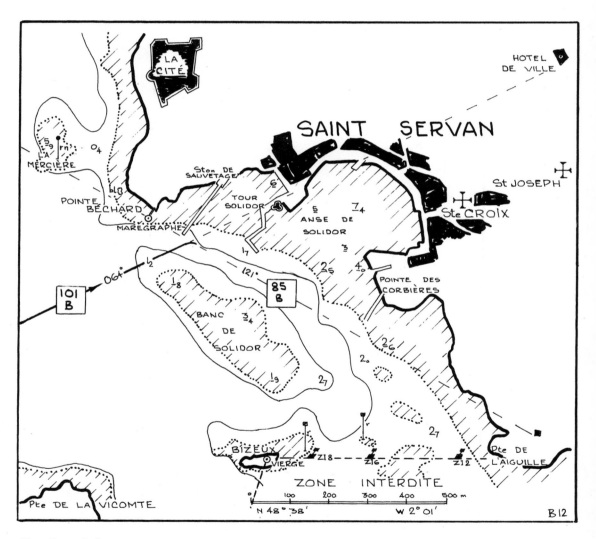

Chart B12—St Servan

112

13—ILE DE CÉZEMBRE

Rather more than a picnic spot—there is a small restaurant here—the anchorage is on chart B13. The approach is from the Chenal de la Petite Porte, line 76B (p. 95),

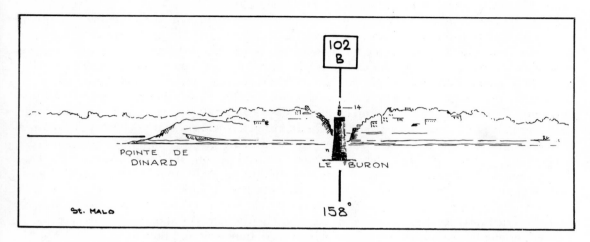

102B   la Vallée de Dinard × le Buron tourelle which leaves les Clefs d'Aval (bouée '10' rouge) a few metres to stb'd.

Chart B13—Ile de Cézembre

113

14—LA RANCE

Would banal be the word to use to describe a cruise to St Malo without sampling the River Rance? If you are untouched by the scenery, if you prefer eating on board, then at least the calm of the anchorages is a contrast to the bustle of St Malo.

Since the recent tidal power station, the entire river has become a vast sailing area with currents less than formerly. Chart B14 shows the lock and the forbidden zone. The Rance is never less than 2·0m above zero and locking through is free. The lock is 13 × 65m, the cill being 2·0m above zero. The access channel from the north is dredged to 2·0m and Ducs d'Albe (circular mooring dolphins) are placed upstream and downstream of the lock gates. These are lit and may be used by waiting craft. Alongside the NE Duc d'Albe there is 1·25m, the SE one had 2·2m. The lock functions day and night, Sundays and holidays, providing there is a 4m tide rise or greater. Opening times are on the hour, provided you present your boat 20 minutes before. Between 2030 and 0430, prior warnings must be given 2 hours before arrival, by telephone (46.21.87). At night the lock-keeper can also be roused by a bellrope on the Duc d'Albe nearest the lock, upstream and downstream but it must be 20 minutes before the hour, as in daylight. An illuminated panel 'Appell Reçu' acknowledges your presence.

A timetable of opening hours, dictated by tide levels, is displayed at: St Malo lock office, St Malo Port de Plaisance, Bas Sablons marina, Châtelier lock and local papers. A free automatic answering telephone number is 46.14.46 which gives the levels and hours.

The signals controlling movements of boats are displayed on a mast on top of the lock building, see also chart B14 'Écluse'. A sphere, a cone point down, and lights are shown thus:

River Rance Lock	Day	Night
Entry forbidden from seaward Entry forbidden from the river	Sphere Cone	Red Light Green Light

The two signals together indicate no movement is permitted. No signals are shown outside opening hours.

If anchoring within a mile of the barrage, not only is there an unpleasant underwater noise of the turbine blades but at certain times there is a disturbance which causes a boat to swing around and possibly break out her anchor. This is caused either by the water through the generating turbines or through the six sluice gates at the eastern end. Two signal masts warn when there is any flow of water in or out of either lots of equipment. The masts are shown on chart B14; one marked 'Usine' is in the centre of the barrage and concerns the turbines; the other is above the sluice gates, marked 'Vannes'.

The day signals are white-above-black cones, points up or black-above-white cones, points down. At night the lights are arranged in vertical pairs. The various hoists are thus:

Turbines or sluice gates	Upstream Flow (Flood)	Downstream Flow (Ebb)
Day	White-over-black cones	Black-over-white cones
Night	Green-above-white lights	White-above-green lights

No signal means no water flow.

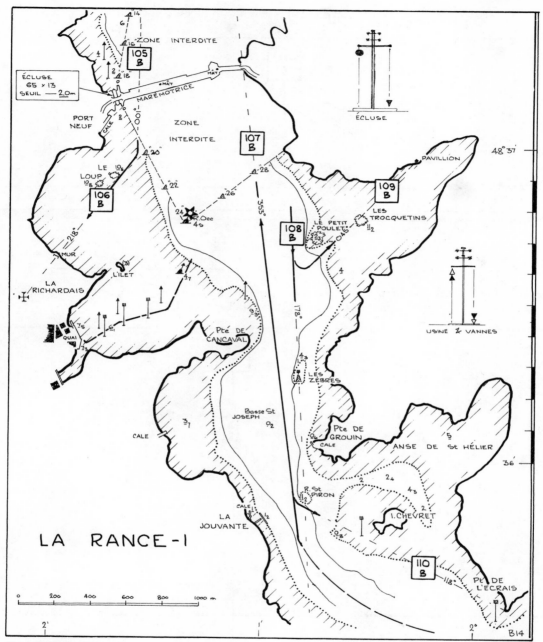

Chart B14—La Rance I

Navigation in the Rance, once through the lock is simple above half tide, see charts B14 and B15 (p. 119). As, however, the levels sometimes fall to 2·0m above zero, pilot marks are then of use in avoiding the several rocks.

French Pilot I

Do not, for example, turn too sharply when leaving the lock going south,

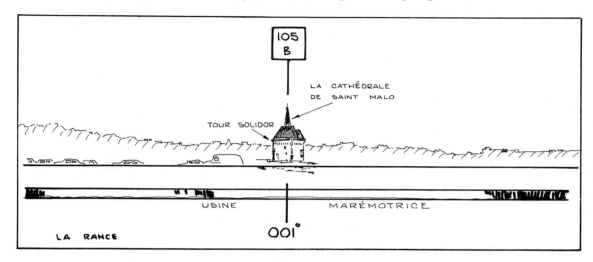

105B   St Malo Cathedral × la Tour Solidor clears to the east of le Loup *10·5m* and if you wish to anchor in the bay just south-west of these rocks, take line

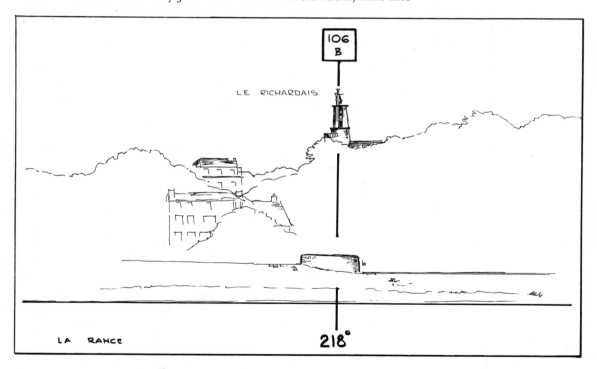

106B   le Richardais Church × a granite wall near the water's edge. The church has a striking crucifix on its spire. This line clears le Loup to the south-east.

Le Richardais is a useful village in which to pass a night; the quay dries 7·3m and the channel is clearly posted all the way from a black buoy 'Richardais'. There is a village shop, a tap on the quay, a slip, grid for scrubbing, and a crane.

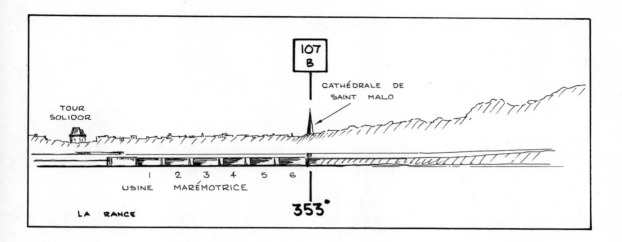

107B   St Malo Cathedral × the sluices is the line to take you right up river. Use the right side of the 6th and last sluice.

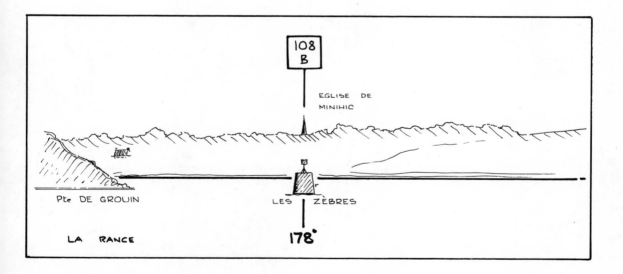

108B   Minihic Church × les Zèbres tourelle is a mark to clear a group of rocks, le Petit Poulet 2·3m to the west. To clear to the south (109B)

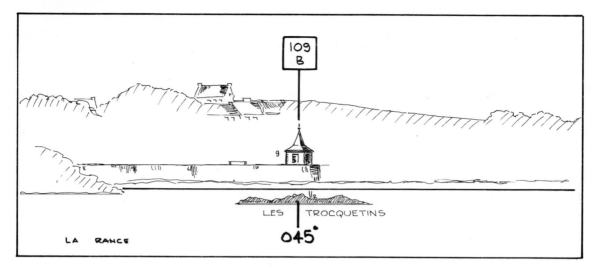

109B   a small stone pavilion × les Trocquetins *11·2m* takes you round and into a quiet bay. If les Trocquetins is covered, then a painful peck from le Poulet is unlikely.

At la Jouvante there is a slip drying *1·0m* at the end and also a mini-marina consisting of some pontoons, *1·2m* on the outside. The English proprietor of a restaurant there kindly provides them for his clients.

Don't turn too sharply near Ile Chevret, Roche St Piron *1·2m* awaits, but line

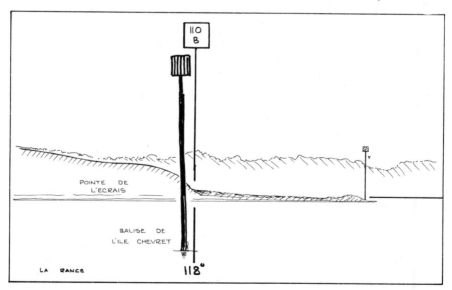

110B   Pointe de l'Ecrais × balise de l'Ile Chevret clears outside. This is in case you want to anchor north of this island where many local boats are kept. On the opposite side of the river to Ile aux Moines lies an interesting bay, sometimes referred to as Landriais but the correct name is Minihic-sur-Rance, see chart B15.

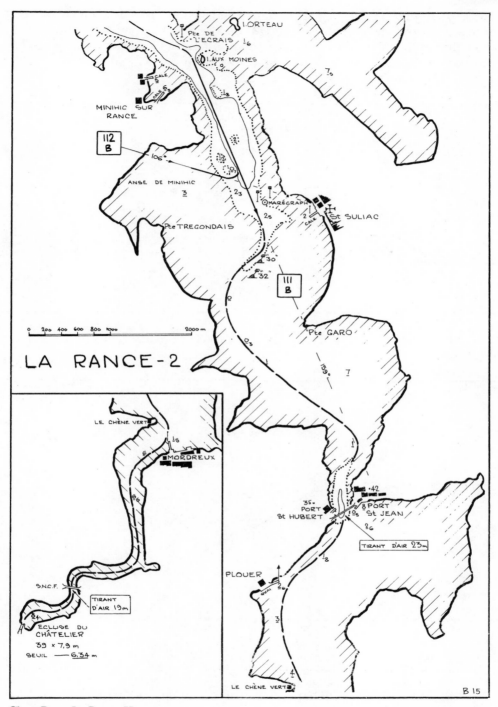

Chart B15—La Rance II

French Pilot I

On the north side is a public slip 5·0m at the end and on the south side a private pontoon. This belongs to a boatyard who don't object to dinghies using it. There is an excellent hard beach nearby for drying out, shops in the village 500m distant. The yard has all repair facilities, electrical and mechanical engineers, and a patent slipway.

The next mid-channel mark is

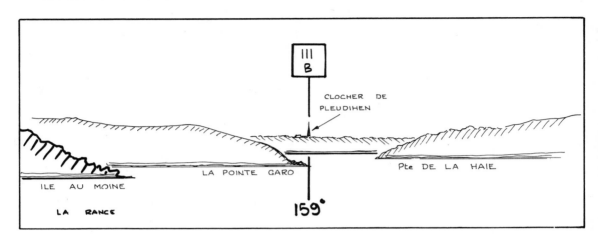

111B   Pleudihen Church × Pointe Garo, which clears rocks drying from 2·0m to 0·7m on both sides until St Suliac is reached. Use line

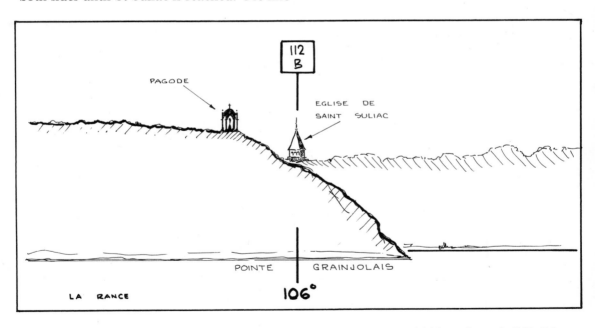

112B   St Suliac Church × Pointe Grainjolais if turning to stb'd into Anse de Minihic to avoid the 0·7m rock.

St Suliac needs no marks and two white posts show the end of the slip which locals swear has always 2m of water. Here is quite a sizeable village with a restaurant, shops, etc.

Here, too, the buoys start, and on going upstream all are port hand, and numbered upwards from No. 30.

The next metropolis is the twin villages of St Hubert and Port St Jean. The second is the important partner which has a most suitable quay drying between 7 and *8m* as well as a slip. The village is a 50m climb, mostly steps, but there is a friendly café at the top. From 2 to 3 cables north of the bridge (rebuilt since the war) is a deep anchorage, 2 to 5 metres, fair holding.

Carrying on upstream there is a most comfortable quay at Plouer terminating in a slip *2·6m* at the end. The quay dries *7·5m* and has a water tap. The village of Plouer-sur-Rance is a kilometre away.

The last village is Mordreux whose middle-ages quay dries up to *7m*. There is a tidal level gauge on the slip, which dries *1·5m*, but is suitable for drying alongside (2·5m high). Village shop only, bread agent at the café.

From here it is 2 miles of well-buoyed channel to the swing bridge and lock at le Châtelier, dimensions on chart B15 (p. 119). The mediaeval town of Dinan is 3 miles along the Canal d'Ille-et-Rance, which has quays on its left bank 600 metres long, with 175 on the opposite bank. The depth in the canal varies with tide and rainfall; 1·5m is supposed to be the least. The depths and times of lock openings may be found at the same place as those of the Rance lock (see p. 114). From Dinan the Canal d'Ille-et-Rance starts off, passing through Rennes and Redon where it joins Canal de Nantes à Brest. As far as Redon the limits are: draught 1·2m, beam 4·5m, height 2·5m. You meet the sea again either at La Roche Bernard (River Vilaine) or at Nantes (River Loire). Neither canal has any commercial traffic.

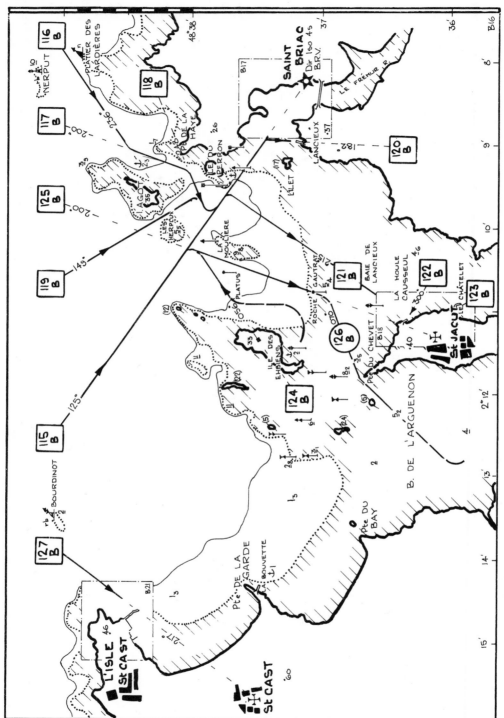

Chart B16—Baie de St Cast

ST BRIAC

The twelve miles from St Malo to Cap Fréhel is mostly dismissed by cruising yachts . . . wide sandy bays, offlying rocks, no harbours worth much, and so on. How about then, adding to your repertoire half a dozen new harbours and anchorages? Most of them are on chart B16.

We'll start with St Briac, a smallish holiday town of 2000 inhabitants. It needs a single mark

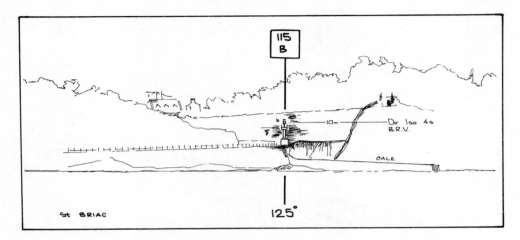

115B the light structure 'Embouchure du Frémur' at 125°. This doesn't sound very helpful, but in fact this recent light is lit 24 hours and has an intensified narrow beam (white 1°) on the required heading. There used to be an old mill but it is completely covered in trees, which served as a back mark. The transit leaves les Herplux *5·5m* a cable to port, la Moulière balise 1½ cables to stb'd, les Perronais balise 50m to port, Bouchot balise 50m to stb'd, le Cheval balise a cable to port, by which time we are on chart B17 and passing two gateways of final balises.

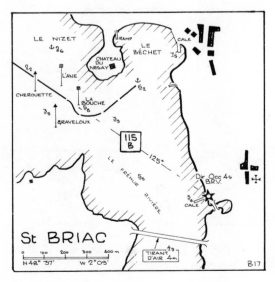

Chart B17—St Briac

French Pilot I

There is a 2·9m anchorage on the above transit and south of Ile du Perron. Another drying 2·6m on firm sand in le Nizet (chart B17, p. 123). A third, among local boats in le Béchet 6·2m. This is the most secure of all and is only 2 minutes from the village. Land at the slip shown as drying 7·5m. There is a tap nearby, a garage within 100m. The rather rickety bridge just upstream of the light hasn't much headroom (4·0m) and through it there is another half mile of clean sand with a rivulet down the centre.

One alternative approach is from St Malo using the Chenal du Décollé and the Passage à Terre de Nerput. In fact line 87B (chart B9, p. 93) takes you a few metres north of the Platier des Lardières (bouée noire). From here take

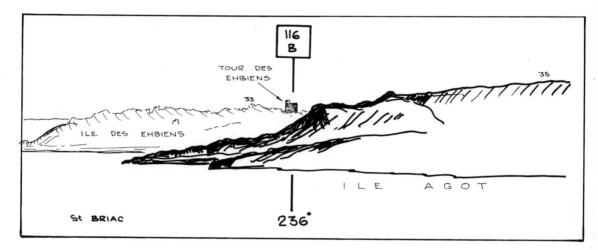

116B   la Tour des Ehbiens (on an island of the same name) × the left side of Ile Agot. When 4 cables off this isle, seek

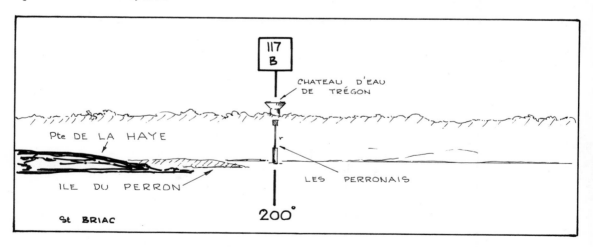

117B   Trégon water-tower × les Perronais balise. At this turn there is a sheltered anchorage, just off the sandy beach on Ile Agot, 2·3m sand. After half a mile,

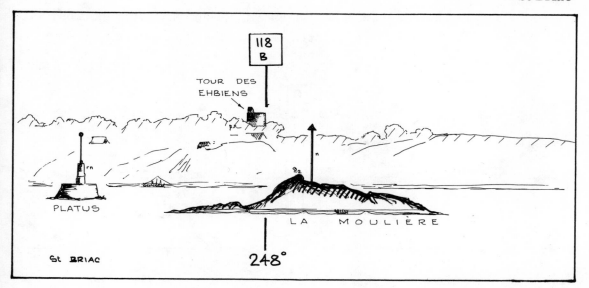

118B   la Tour des Ehbiens × la Moulière balise, which joins the main transit 115B (p. 123).
To pass inside les Herflux and Ile Agot where there is 1·3m,

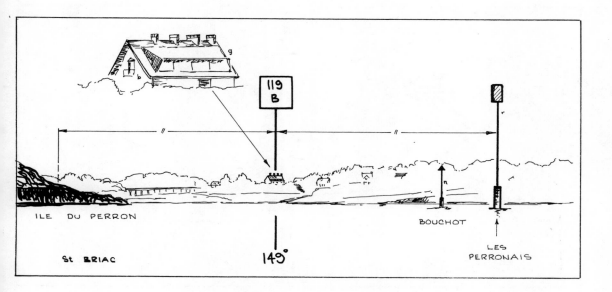

119B   a house, with four distinctive chimneys, midway between the high water mark on Ile due Perron and les Perronais balise. This joins 118B.

125

French Pilot I

Another anchorage is on the south of Ile des Ehbiens; a private island. From the main transit 115B (p. 123), look for a stern mark.

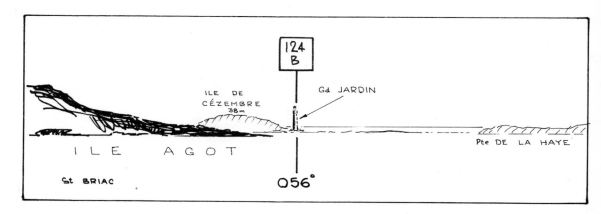

124B Ile de Cézembre × the right side of Ile Agot. When past Platus balise (on 125B, p. 130) a cable to port, make for the small bay in Ehbiens.

LANCIEUX

Returning to the main transit 115B (p. 123), why not branch off to stb'd along line

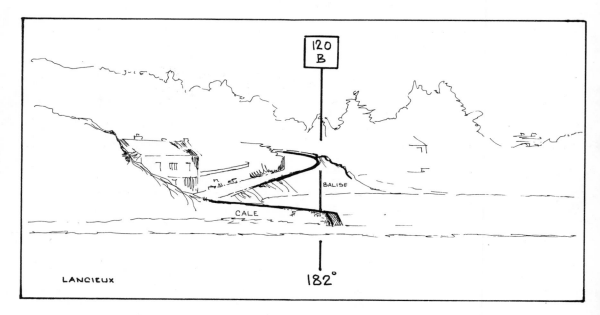

120B Lancieux, the right hand bend in the road × a post at the end of the slip. Between the slip and l'Ilet it is much used by local yachts; it's all sand. A shop is about 250m away.

126

LA HOULE CAUSSEUL

Returning to our much used line 115B (p. 123), there is a nice short cut to the next bay, Baie de Lancieux, wide and sandy. From Ile du Perron,

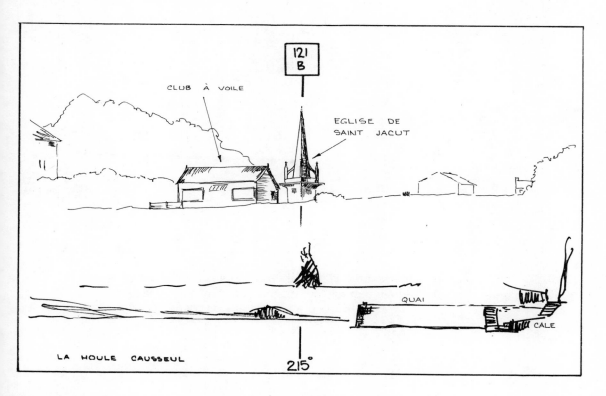

121B   St Jacut Church × the yacht club. The spire is distinctive, but the club could not be described without offending its members, see chart B18 (p. 128). Pass 50m to the east of la Charbotière balise (CE) and right in front there is a tiny quay with a large name, la Houle Causseul.

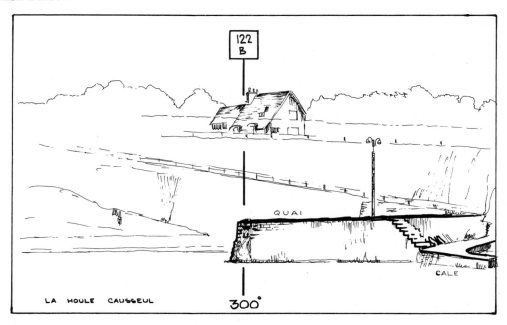

LA HOULE CAUSSEUL   300°

122B   is the entrance mark and it clears all obstructions, a large house × the end of the quay. The quay is small and low, best dry out on the flat, hard sand nearby.

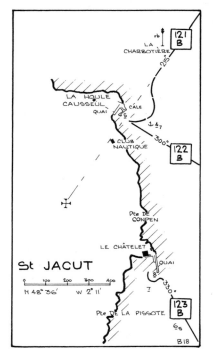

Chart B18—St Jacut

LE CHÂTELET

Now that you are here you might as well try another genuine harbour, le Châtelet, hardly half a mile southward. The entrance is

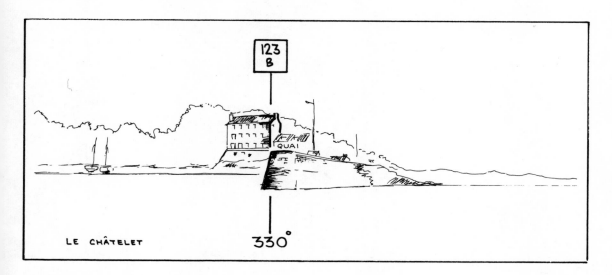

123B   so easy that my sketch serves to illustrate this vast port. It is the large house × the end of the quay. Neither of these two harbours has any facilities but they are really the ports serving St Jacut (pop. 1100) only 500m up the hill.

LE GUILDO

Still once more taking our departure from our old friend line 115B (p. 123), here is the passage further west into Baie de l'Arguenon.

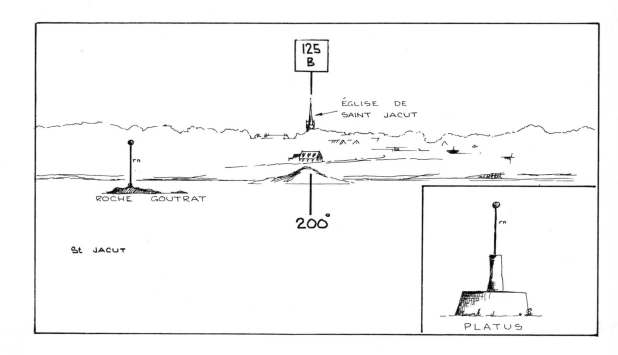

125B   St Jacut Church × a house north of la Houle, which leaves la Moulière balise 1½ cables to port, Platus balise 60m to stb'd. A mile down this mark and when abreast of Roche Gautrat balise (danger isolé) use it on a stern bearing

126B   (no view) of 070°. This bearing passes midway between Pointe du Chevet and le Petit Anon balise (CE) a cable wide gap. At this point steer south-west so as to leave la Petite Roche 5·0m high a cable to stb'd, and so out into Baie de l'Arguenon, and in to the channel which dries 4·7m and now, since the tide is rising, is the time to explore your way up to le Guildo, a Romano-Celtic village.

Chart B19 takes over here—there are no navigational hazards—the whole bay is sand, sand, sand. I'm sorry I can't give you a proper sketch of the south end of the bay, but it appears on no French charts. However, I've a plan of the village, chart B20 showing the balises. At low water all is mud, with a rivulet in the channel, Rivière de l'Arguenon. There are drying berths along the north side where I show a 5·6m sounding. Tap on quay, fuel, and everything found in a village of about 1000. There is even a Douane on the quay so there must be occasional maritime activity, though I have never seen much. Many relics of the Roman occupation abound. They built several forts here, no doubt attracted by the mineral springs at Sassay.

Le Guildo

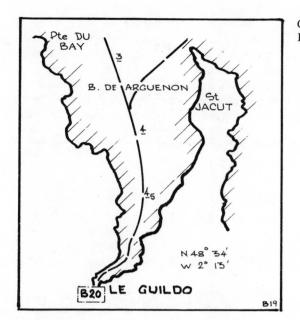

Chart B19—
Baie de l'Arguenon

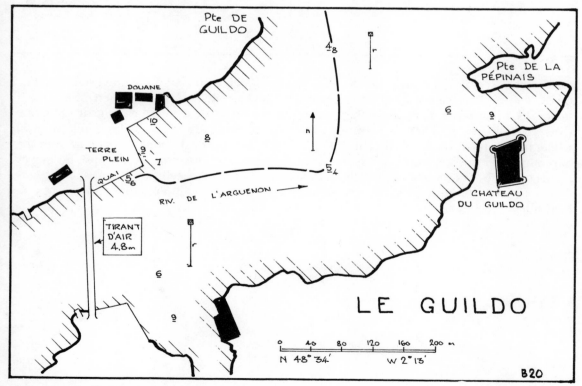

Chart B20—Le Guildo

ST CAST

Still on chart B16 (p. 122), and sailing out of Baie de l'Arguenon north-westward, a convenient overnight anchorage is just short of Pointe de la Garde. Many local boats are moored off a slip at la Bouvette where a steep walk of 1½km takes you into St Cast town.

The Port of St Cast however is a mile to the north, on chart B21, and is in process of expansion. The approach from the east needs no marks but coming in from the north there is a rock of 2·6m so, from a position a couple of cables west of le Bourdinot (bouée CE)

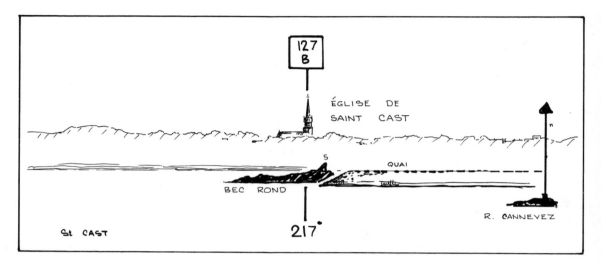

127B   St Cast Church × Bec Rond, a 5m high rock with a white painted summit. The rock can just be seen clear of the end of the new breakwater which I'm told is not to be extended further. Fishing boats monopolise the 1·5m quay but there are drying berths near the crane where *6·0m* is shown. There is normally ample room west of the Cale de la Feuillâtre *4·7m* where fishing boats often scrub. The long black building marked 'Douane' contains also the harbourmaster's office, showers, telephones and chandlery. There are water taps and power points on the quays, in fact the whole port has had a complete face lift.

St Cast has a whimsical monument showing a French greyhound making mincemeat of a British leopard.

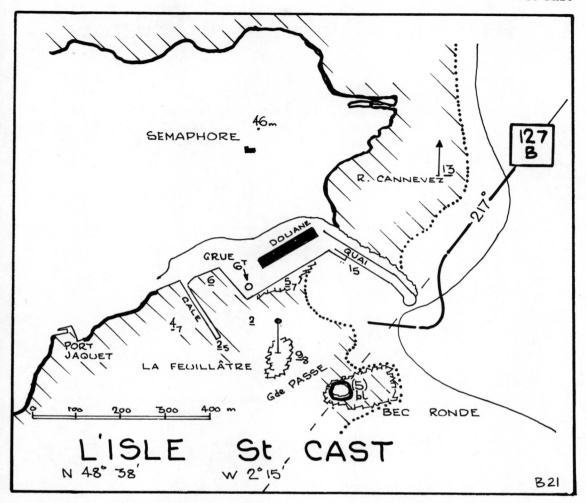

Chart B21—L'Isle St Cast

C Baie de la Fresnaie to Tréguier

BAIE DE LA FRESNAIE

Before rounding our next major headland, Cap Fréhel, there is the third and last of those large sandy bays, Fresnaie. Largely a mussel and oyster area this bay is enclosed by 50m cliffs with trees and grass down to the tide mark. On chart C1, half a mile from the road bridge at the head of the bay lies a beautiful old stone harbour, well preserved and with a flat sandy bottom—Port Nieux.

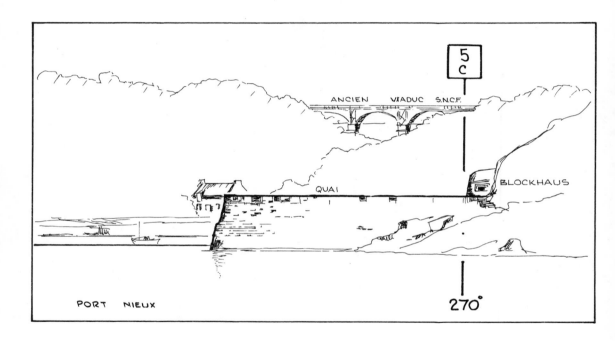

5C   shows the quay and a slightly needless mark, the right end of a fine disused railway bridge × a horrible, also disused, German blockhaus. There are good berths alongside to the west of the miniscule quay. Apart from a child playing outside the only house and a nesting thrush, there seemed little else when we dried out there. You did say you wished to cruise? Not just marina to marina?

If Port Nieux's pace is too hectic, try Port St Géran, a mile and a half north, chart C1. Here I fell into a discussion with two octogenarian fishermen about the exact name of their port. It's only a pair of slips anyway—no shops within a thousand miles.

A bit further up the bay, and well worth a visit, is Fort de la Latte

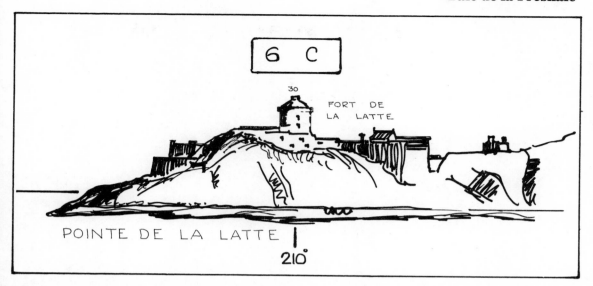

6C (view only) and there is a safe anchorage just south of the fort. This 13th century stronghold was restored recently, about 1600. It had then a cannon-ball foundry, the appearance of which would warm any trade-unionist's heart. The landing is on the south-east side below the drawbridge. The buoy (danger isolé) half a mile SE of the fort marks the drying wreck of the steamship 'Laplace'.

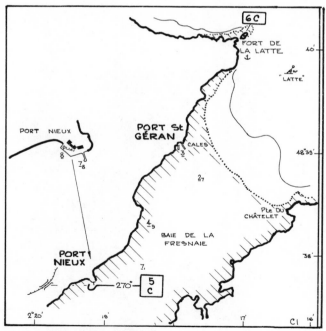

Chart C1—Baie de la Fresnaie

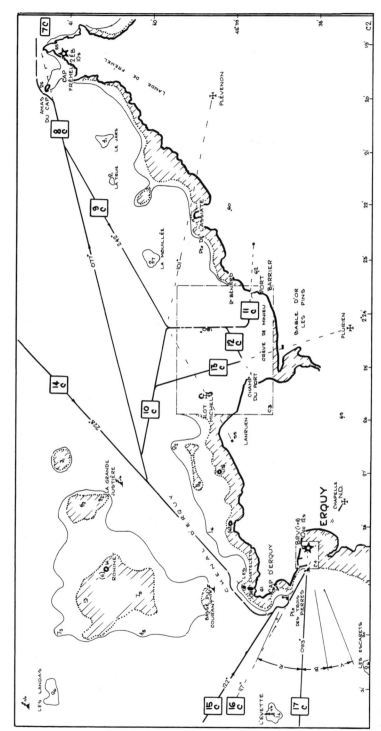

Chart C2 — De Cap Fréhel à Erquy

PORT BARRIER

Rounding Cap Fréhel is no problem, it is steep-to (a cable off is 16m). The tides here and as far west as the Chenal d'Erquy are regular. The flood starts at St Malo — 0520 hrs to the ENE at 3 knots; and the ebb at +0020 hrs to the WSW at 2·5 knots. These spring rates can be cut by a third at neaps.

Chart C2 covers the next part of the rather sparsely populated coast as far as Erquy.

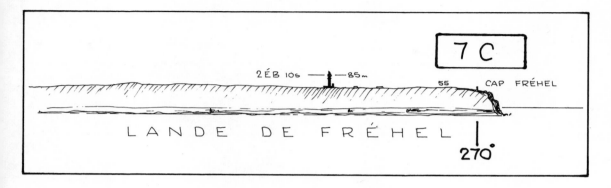

7C shows a view of Cap Fréhel (270°); don't approach it from the east on a greater bearing, there are some shoals, la Roche de l'Etendrée *3·9m* ½ mile to the ESE. Though deep, there is little point in sailing between the Cap and Amas du Cap, and as soon as round the latter come onto the main coastwise mark

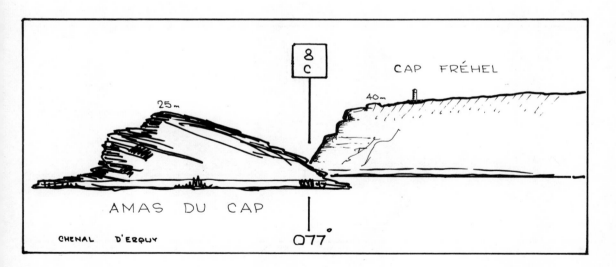

8C the cliff of Cap Fréhel × the right side of Amas du Cap which leads into the Chenal d'Erquy. But before this there are a couple of small harbours in Grève de Minieu. The eastern approach is (9C)

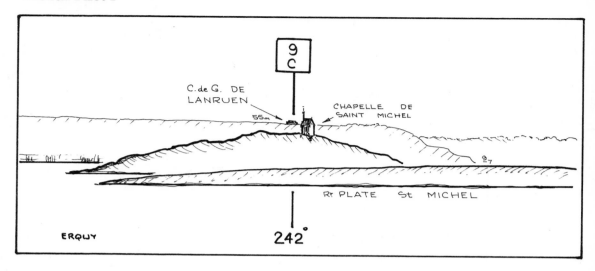

9C Lanruen Coast Guard × Chapelle de St Michel, both are quite unmistakeable and the mark clears to seaward of le Jars, la Truie and la Mouillée. A breast mark which is also the approach mark from the west is

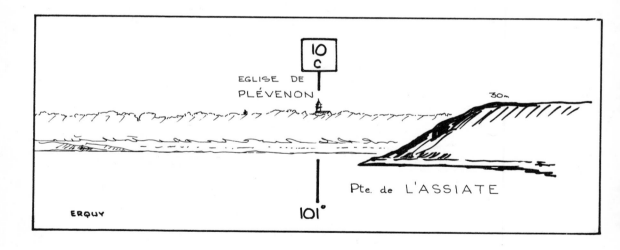

10C Plévenon Church open to the left of Pointe de l'Assiate. When these two transits cross, aim south and take the choice of two harbours.

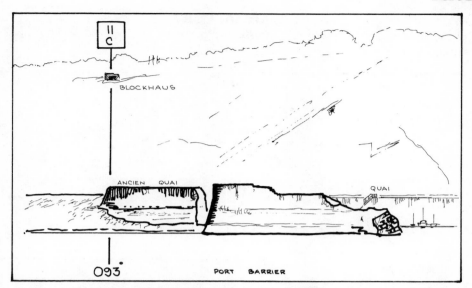

11C   Port Barrier, a German blockhaus × the extreme left of the ruined quay. This is a disused quarry harbour, on chart C3, providing a flat sandy bottom for drying out alongside, between $5\cdot5m$ and $6\cdot5m$. Naturally there are no facilities, but in summer the holiday town of Sables d'Or les Pins comes to life, half a mile away.

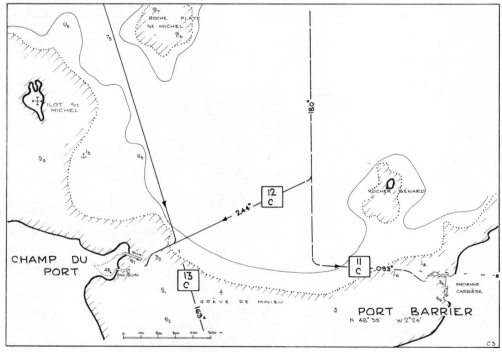

Chart C3—Port Barrier and Champ du Port

139

CHAMP DU PORT

The other harbour is more interesting; Champ du Port was also a quarry port but now shelters a few fishing boats.

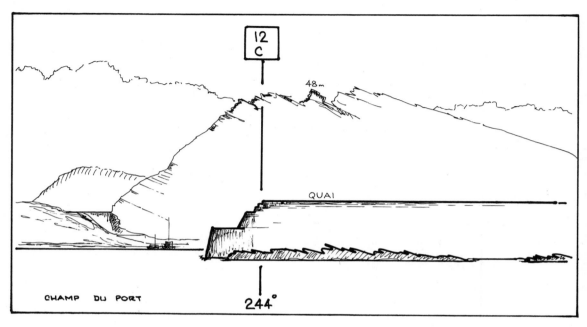

12C Champ du Port, a high hill backing the harbour × the end of the quay. No facilities here either, except ice creams in summer, but a comfortable lean against the granite quay. There is a channel

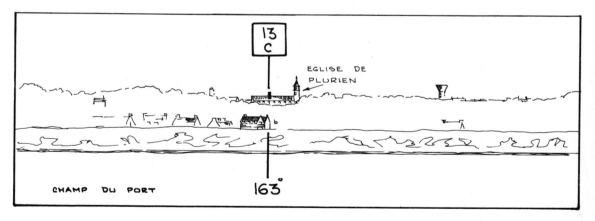

13C Plurien Church × the last of a row of houses on the dunes, which leads between la Roche Plate and Ilot St Michel. Between the Chapelle and Champ du Port is good anchorage while waiting for the tide in the Chenal d'Erquy, but watch out for the *0·9m* rock just west of line 13C.

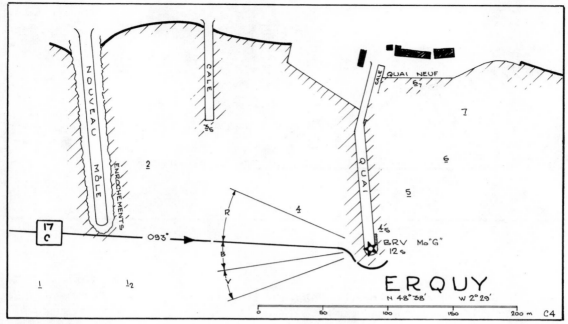

Chart C4—Erquy

ERQUY

Back now to chart C2 (p. 136), Chenal d'Erquy lies between four square miles of rocks dominated by a central whitened rock, Rohinet, and the mainland.

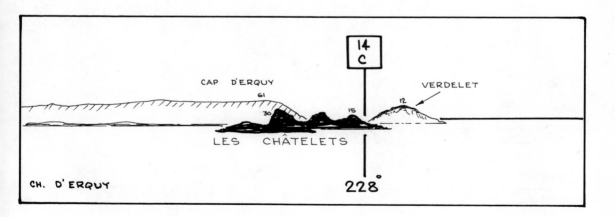

14C   Verdelet × the right side of les Châtelets leaves Justières (bouée CS) 2 cables to stb'd and when abreast of Basses du Courant (bouée CS) make a handrail to the west of Cap d'Erquy. There are several dangerous rocks but if you want to cut it fine, the clearance is (15C)

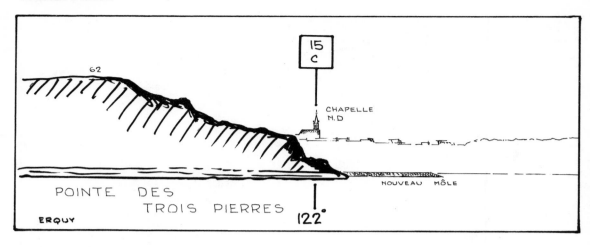

15C   la Chapelle Notre Dame × Pointe des Trois Pierres. This mark can be seen many miles out which the following one can't.

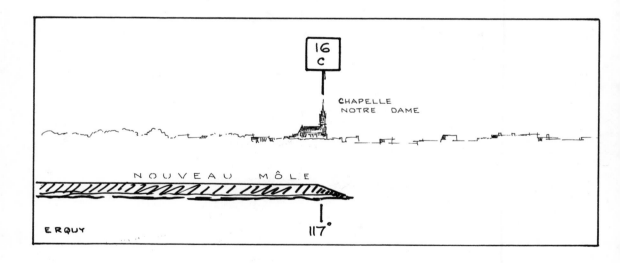

16C   the same Chapelle Notre Dame × the end of the new breakwater. The west approach is on chart C4 (p. 141) also.

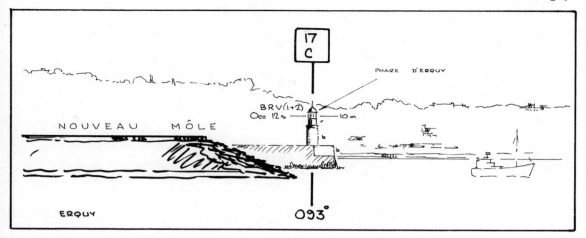

17C   Erquy light × the end of the breakwater. This is the only safe night approach, using the white sector. The line 17C clears south of l'Evette (tourelle CN).

Erquy is an important fishing port, though unfortunately facing west. The new mole cannot be used for coming alongside and its eastern shelter is packed with fishermen. They use the slip between the west (new) and the east (old) breakwaters. The best berths are to the east of the light or alongside the Quai Neuf. Least trouble is to put down two legs and dry out in hard, level sand NE of the light about the sounding *6m* or *7m*, but bow and stern anchors must be used to lie parallel with the many fishing boats. It has all the amenities of a fishing port—including fish!

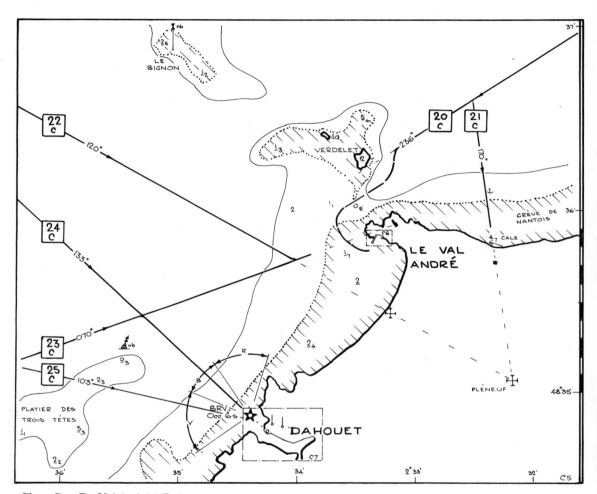

Chart C5—Du Val André à Dahouet

LE VAL ANDRÉ

Between Erquy and the next two harbours, le Val André and Dahouet and nearly a mile out from Grève de Nantois, lie many drying rocks, and to clear these to seaward line

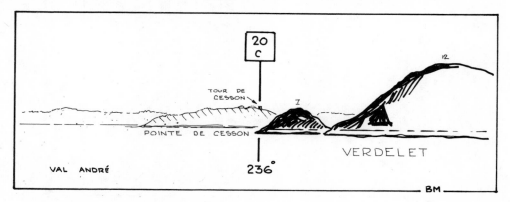

20C   Tour de Cesson (St Brieuc) × the left of le Verdelet. The far mark is 10 miles off. We should now be on chart C5 and in order to reach the above two harbours you can either take a five mile detour north of Plateau des Jaunes and le Bignon balise (CW) or cut between le Verdelet and the mainland. The route lies about mid-channel and carries 0·5m or say 4·2m at MLW neaps.

But before doing so, try

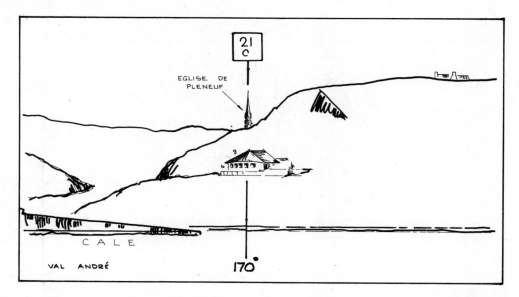

21C   Pleneuf Church × a distinctive house on the cliffs. This has a large conical roof, and the line leads into a *4·7m* drying quay. More important, I once saw a couple of large schooners sheltering there during a brisk southwesterly—at the time Erquy, Dahouet and le Val André were dry.

145

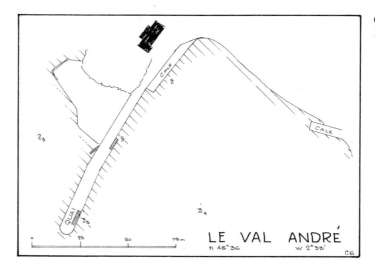

Chart C6—
Le Val André

Once through the inside passage of Verdelet, give a couple of cables offing and enter le Val André. The harbour, all flat and sandy, on chart C6 isn't used by fishing boats and berths can usually be found alongside the quay. The full name of this holiday resort is Pléneuf-Val-André (population 4000) but none of its facilities seems to have much to do with the sea. Its port is really Dahouet, a mile away.

An alternative approach from the NW and to avoid all the dangers to seaward of Verdelet is line

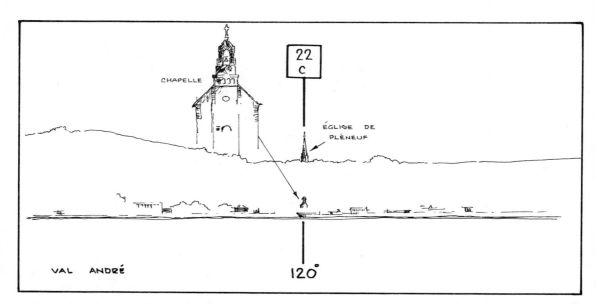

22C   Pléneuf Church × a chapelle near the water. Coming in from the west to keep to seaward of all the rocks off le Platier des Trois Têtes, use

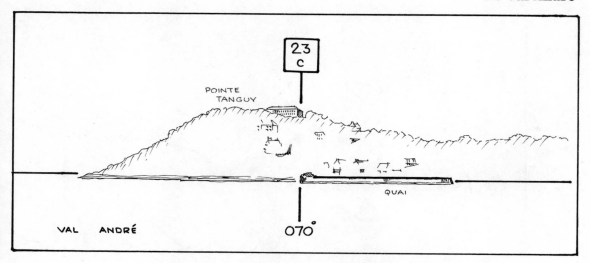

23C the right side of a vast hotel on Pte. Tanguy × the left end of the quay. The same mark is used in approaching Dahouet from the west.

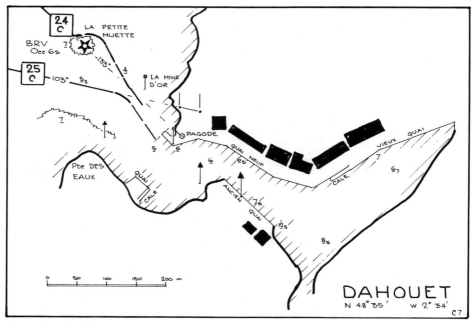

Chart C7—Dahouet

DAHOUET

Last of all on chart C5 (p. 144) is a genuine old port, snug, used by fishing boats, easy to enter—
Dahouet. A close-up is on chart C7.

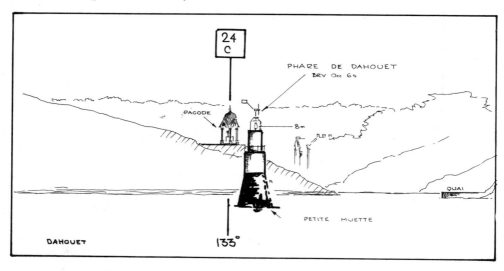

24C   is the usual entrance, a pagoda × la Petite Muette light. When 50m from this light
make a handrail to the east and leave la Mine d'Or balise 25m to port and head for the slip, with
a post. (No topmark.)

148

If there is enough water, you may pass to the south of la Petite Muette using

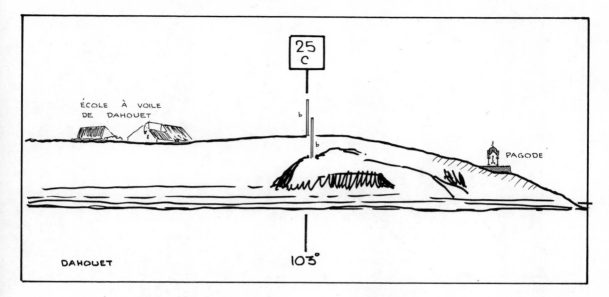

25C   a pair of white poles in line. This passage is over level rock, so make sure of the tidal rise—it dries *5·2m*. This part is incidentally covered with mussels; 10 minutes with a bucket at low water should help you to appreciate Dahouet.

The Quai Neuf is mostly occupied by fishing boats but the Vieux Quai, from the slip eastward, is excellent for leaning against. The Ancien Quai is, as the name suggests, useless, but many yachts winter at the south end *8·5m* in mud berths. There is water on the quays, fuel, a yacht club, restaurants and cafés full of fishermen.

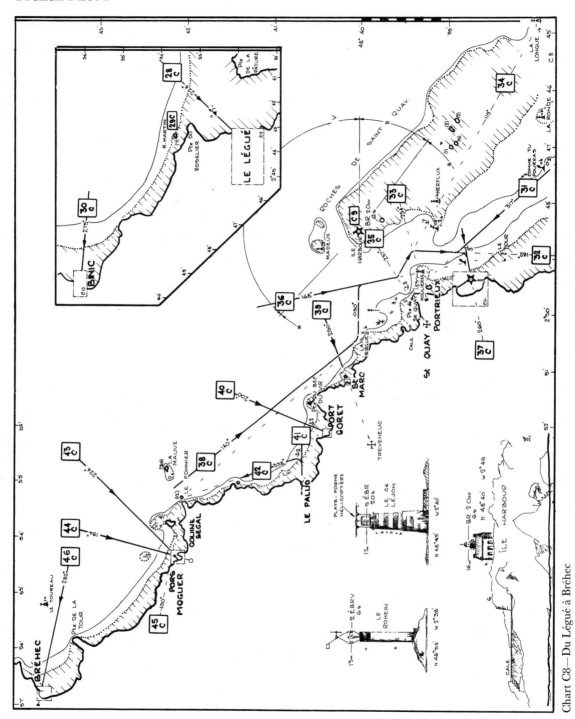

Chart C8—Du Légué à Bréhec

LE LÉGUÉ

With the exception of a couple of oyster quays there is nothing now until l'Anse d'Yffiniac at the west side of which lies le Légué, the port for a large town, St Brieuc. Chart C8 covers the 15 miles of coast from there to Bréhec. On it are views of le Rohein, le Grande Léjon and Ile Harbour.

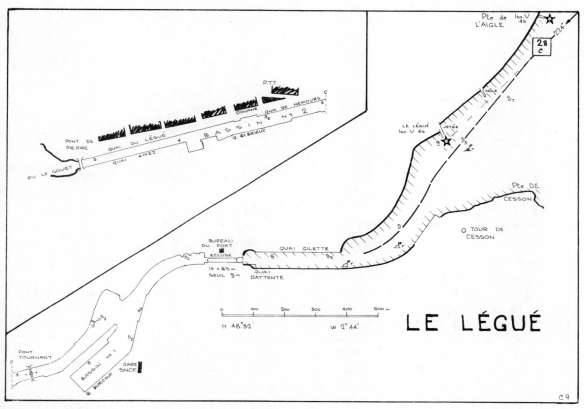

Chart C9—Le Légué

Few yachts visit le Légué since it is a little out of the way when hurrying to the west, but it is an interesting region, and it is possible to lock in to a wet basin. There is a buoyed channel, starting with Bouée No. '1' but after that there is half a mile or more of wilderness, so better take line

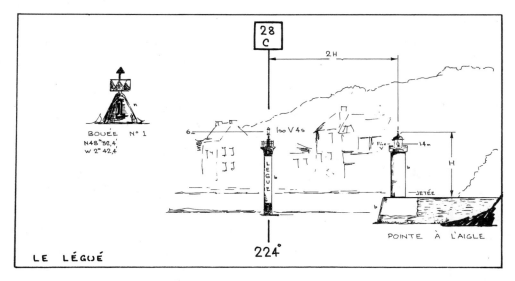

LE LÉGUÉ

28C   a new back light le Légué × Pointe à l'Aigle light. The lights must be opened about 2 heights. When abreast of the front light, now on chart C9 (p. 151), take the approximate track shown. By night use the same pair of lights.

Le Quai Gilette is reserved for commercial craft, but may be used while waiting for the lock gates to open. These operate from St Malo − 2 hours to + 1 hour at springs, but + and − 1 hour at neaps. Ask at the Bureau du Port for a berth—there are plenty—and very likely you will be sent to Quai de Nemours. This is in the town centre, and alongside the Douane, the port office, the square and all shops. Showers nearby, fuel also and plenty of buses up to the main town, St Brieuc. St Brieuc founded the colony in the the 5th century, holding a race meeting some years later on the sands outside the present lock. A boy jockey, son of St Brieuc's A.D.C. was dismounted and hit his head on the only stone in the entire bay, an untimely end to a near win. On still frosty nights at low water his mount's hoofbeats can be clearly heard. If you don't believe me, come with me north to Binic, but pausing at Rocher Martin

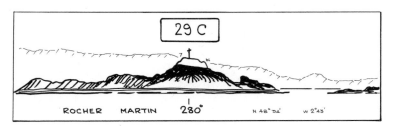

29C   (view only) which I have drawn for useful recognition. The cross on the whitened summit commemorates the young jockey's exploit. See?

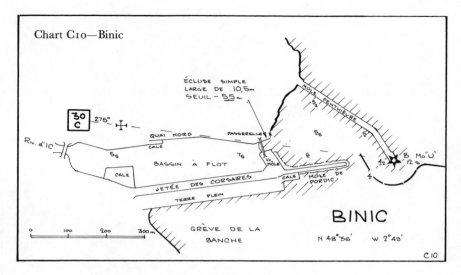

BINIC

A hundred years ago some 50 fishing boats left from Binic to the Iceland grounds for cod. Now the port lives again, but on tourists and has turned her wet basin into a marina for plaisanciers. One mark

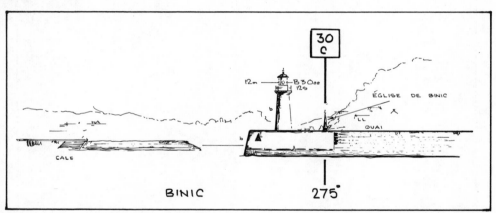

30C is enough, more to show the entrance than anything else, the church × Binic light. Chart C10 shows the port and excellent drying berths are alongside the Môle Penthièvre. Whilst there is perfect shelter inside the basin the opening of the single gate, and sliding bridge, is somewhat restricted. It is supposed to operate at levels above MHW Neaps where here is 8·7m, which gives 3·2m over the cill. I think the lockmaster's meal times, working hours, feast days must also be taken into account. His office is adjacent to the lock gate. On the north side of the lock gate a 6m mast with two horizontal lights controls traffic;

By Day A flag, St Andrew's cross, black on white ground, denotes that the gate is open.

By Night   White + red   — No entry
                    White + green   — No exit
                    Red + green   — No movements

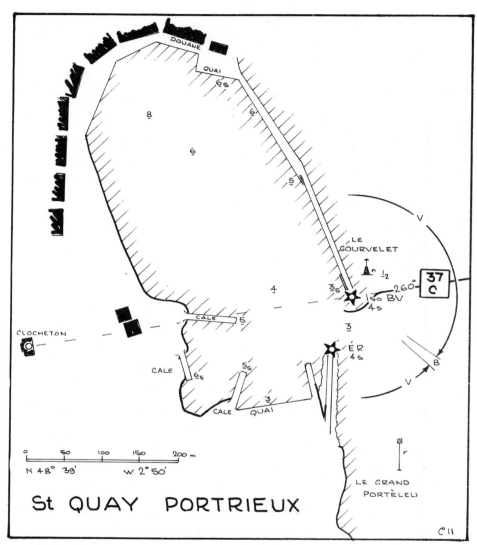

Chart C11—St Quay Portrieux

ST QUAY PORTRIEUX

Coasting northwards you must either stand out some 5 miles to clear les Roches de St Quay or take a well marked inshore channel past the entrance to our next harbour, St Quay Portrieux. We shall take the channel first, then come back to St Quay. Still on chart C8 (p. 150).

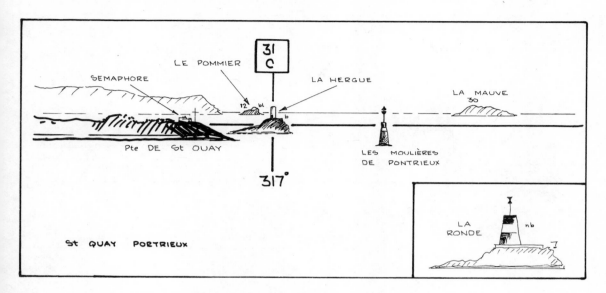

31C   le Pommier × la Hergue tourelle is the leading-in mark. Le Pommier is over 7 miles from Binic but has a whitened summit. This line leaves la Rosellière (bouée CW) 2 cables to stb'd, la Ronde (tourelle CW) ½ mile to stb'd, Comme tu Pourras (bouée CE) ½ cable to stb'd, le Four (tourelle blanche) 4 cables to port. When abreast of St Quay entrance take a stern mark

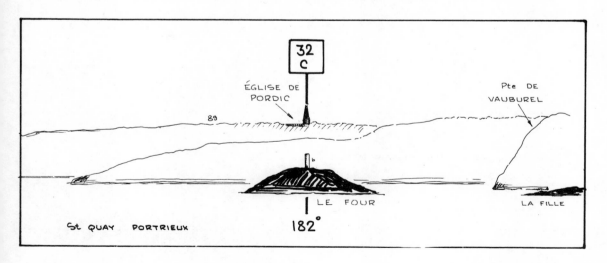

32C   Pordic Church × le Four tourelle until a port breast mark comes up (33C)

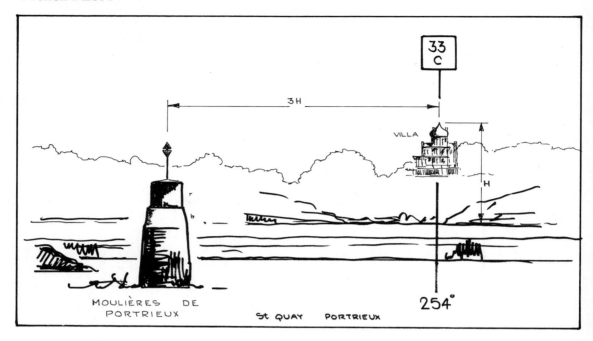

33C   a villa (like the Taj Mahal) 3 times its height to the right of les Moulières de Portrieux (tourelle CE),

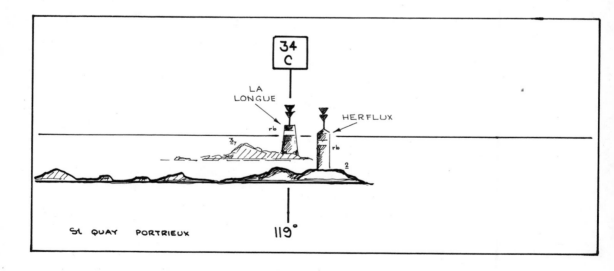

34C   la Longue and Herflux (tourelles CS) until the next port breast mark,

156

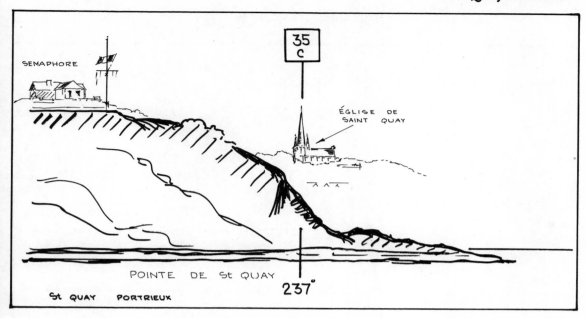

35C St Quay Church × the cliff below the semaphore. Next a stern mark

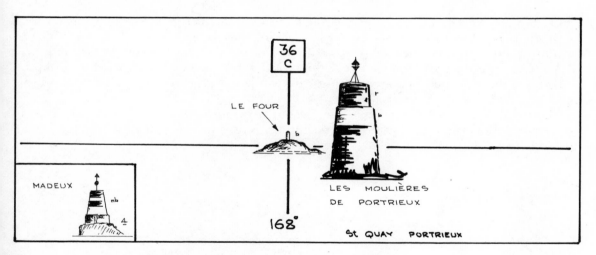

36C le Four (tourelle blanche) × les Moulières (tourelle CE) which takes you out to sea again.

Now return to line 31C and the St Quay entrance, where there is an excellent anchorage in 1·8m sand, halfway between le Gourvelot (chart C11, p. 154) and les Moutons (bouée CE).

The tides in the channel above, by the way, start to run NW at les Héaux de Bréhat HW, maximum speed of 1·9 knots; and to run SE at −5 hours, maximum 2·2 knots. These spring rates are halved at neaps.

French Pilot I

On chart C11 (p. 154), is our entrance mark to St Quay Portrieux

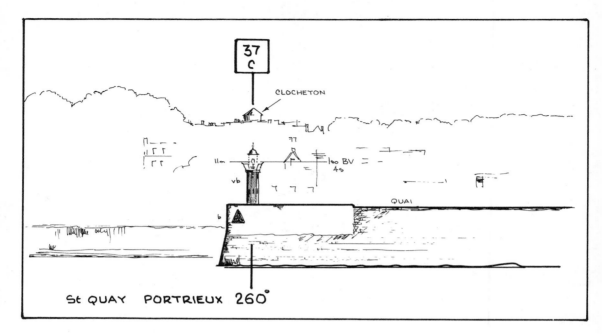

St QUAY PORTRIEUX 260°

37C   a turret × St Quay light. Sail round the quay and there is a vast drying area. Most of the quay between the light northward to sounding *5·0m* is used by trawlers, but from *6m* onward it is mostly free. The cross-berth near the douane *6·5m* is excellent. At the south the E–W berth *3m* is reserved for commercial ships, but yachts may use the adjacent three slips.

By night the only route is from the south-east, within the white sector of the St Quay jetty light.

The town is in two parts; Portrieux—the harbour area, and St Quay—the real town, one km to the north. But everything for the tired yachtsman is near the harbour; water on the quay, fuel, municipal showers, yacht club, launderette.

ST MARC

For seven miles northward there are craggy headlands, coves, bays, and a succession of tiny harbours. Start just alongside la Hergue with the coastal mark

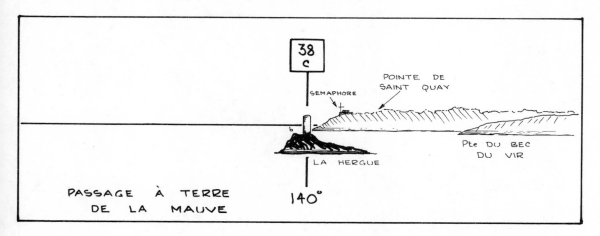

38C   Pointe de St Quay × la Hergue. Not only does this line take you up the coast but eventually leads inside la Mauve. However, here is the first one—well, it's hardly a harbour. St Marc it's called,

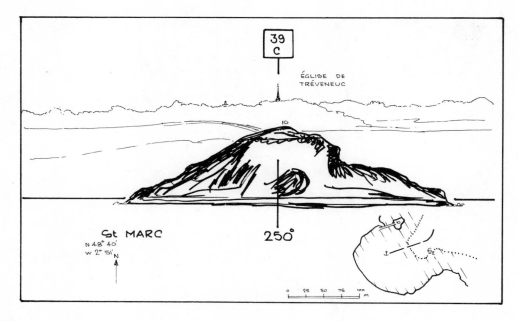

39C   Tréveneuc Church × a 10m high rock. The harbour hides behind this stone, leave it to stb'd, but not more than 30m. There is a tiny quay and some oyster activity, with swinging room for a dozen boats. No room? All right, try the next one.

PORT GORET

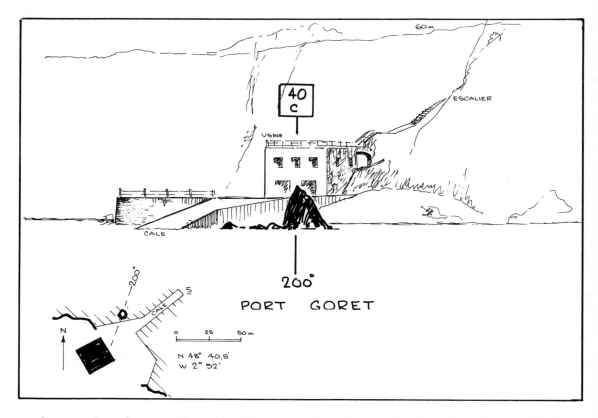

40C   Port Goret, a disused building × a pinnacle rock. Rather gloomy and a climb up several hundred steps, a bit too much? Next please.

LE PALUD

41C le Palud. Make one line with the south face of several houses. What more do you want? Two slips, a sandy beach, a km stroll to the village of Tréveneuc, perfect shelter from the prevailing wind. If you leave in a hurry there are some rocks $1.4m$ near the entrance, but a clearance mark is

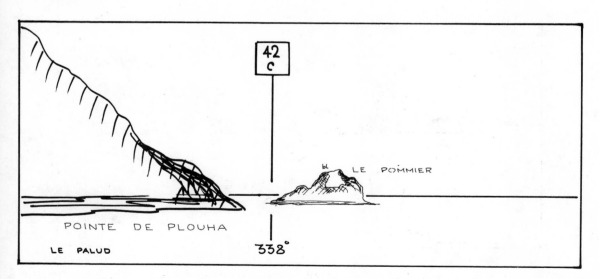

42C le Pommier, now only $1\frac{1}{2}$ miles away × Pointe de Plouha.

GOUINE SEGAL

You can resume line 38C on p. 159, pass between la Mauve and le Pommier where there is 9·0m, and pick out the marks for a real beauty of an anchorage—Gouine Segal. The entrance lies between two marks, each to clear rocks. The SE mark is

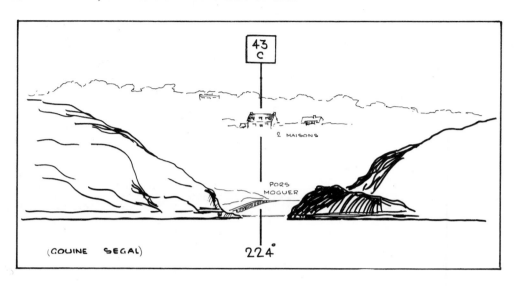

43C   a house at Pors Moguer × the slip. The house is the left of two. The NW mark is

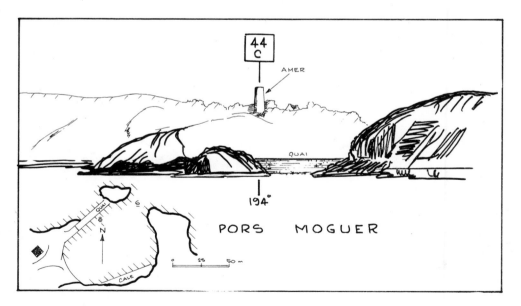

44C   L'Amer de Pors Moguer × the left end of a quay wall. From here there is a choice of Pors Moguer, plan on view 44C or a couple of cables east to Gouine Segal,

162

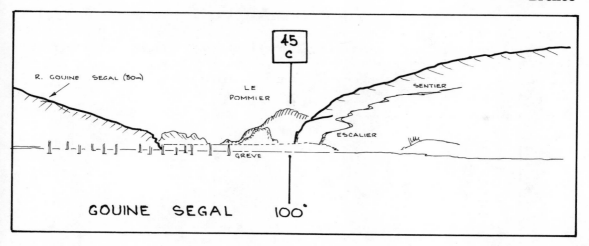

GOUINE SEGAL 100°

45C le Pommier seen just clear of the cliff, which is the mark for anchoring in about 1·5m. A path and steps lead up the cliff but I can't say where to. Many local boats moor to stakes, shown on 45C.

BRÉHEC

The last harbour on this sheltered coast is Bréhec, so easy to enter a transit is hardly needed. However, take

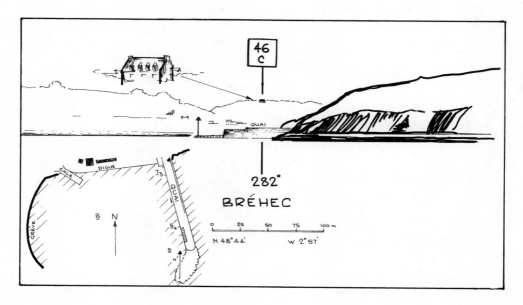

BRÉHEC
282°

N 48°44′   W 2°57′

46C a large house × the root of the stone quay. Recently an extension has been made to the quay, and the drying berths inside, alongside the quay, are excellent, hard sand. Fishing boats are absent but there is a grocer, two restaurants and a bus to Paimpol.

ROCHES DOUVRES

Enough of this skulking in small harbours, let's get away out to sea so that we can really appreciate Ile de Bréhat, Lézardrieux, and Paimpol when we return. So by contrast come with me 25 miles northward, 40–50–60 metres deep—to the Roches Douvres.

There are no detailed charts, the best being French chart 831 ; scale 45,000, but the approach is simple and from the SSW line

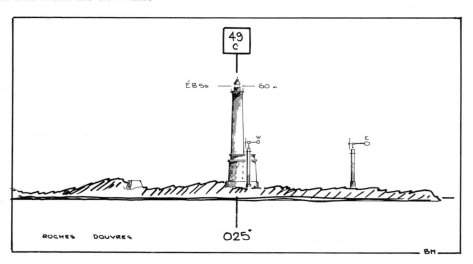

49C   the lighthouse × the left hand wind generator which clears the west rocks off Barnouic. When about 3 cables off the main islet come to the east until

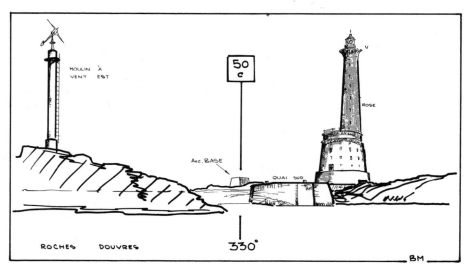

50C   an old concrete foundation in the middle of the small harbour. Anchor where shown or go alongside. There is a slip on the west side if you prefer it ; no marks are required, but simply head north just off the main rock, line

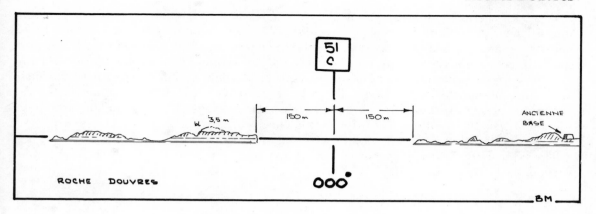

51C (360°) and anchor in line with this slip as shown.

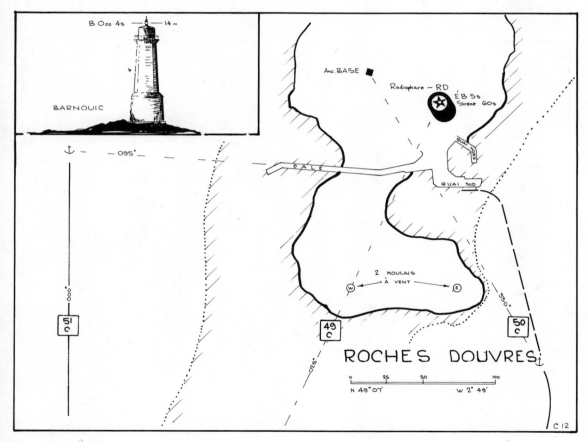

Chart C12—Roches Douvres

French Pilot I

When I first cruised in Brittany, just after the war, the light was carried on a temporary steel tower—the base remains in view 50C (p. 164). The new lighthouse is palatial; take some newspapers and greens and the keepers will make you welcome. It was when I passed once and spied a large vessel alongside—the relief ship—that I realised that there is a quayside there. Chart C12 (p. 165) was drawn using our lead-line as a surveyor's chain, so don't complain if it is an inch or two out. The north quay is useless, all rocks, as is the space between the two quays. The only berth is alongside the south quay, where there is a ladder. The bottom is shingle, and quite suitable for a night stop during neaps. But do not, I beg, tell the travel agents about it when you get back to civilisation or there will soon be a second high-rise building in no time.

The tides are quite fierce, so much so that I give a table for the area between Roches and Barnouic. Reference port—St Malo.

	$+1$	$+3$	$+5$	-5	-3	-1
Direction	—	$300°$	$285°$	$250°$	$110°$	$120°$
Spring rate, knots	slack	3·3	3·7	0·4	4·2	2·9
Neap rate, knots	slack	1·5	1·6	0·2	1·9	1·3

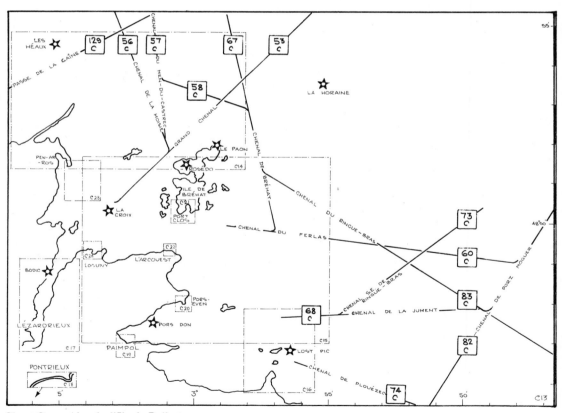

Chart C13—Abords d'Ile de Bréhat

PAIMPOL, LÉZARDRIEUX, ILE DE BRÉHAT

We now come to the most northerly part of Brittany, dominated by two typical river valleys—Tréguier and Trieux. The indented coast is well marked, often with deep channels and the pilotage is correspondingly interesting. Lézardrieux, Ile de Bréhat and Paimpol are all really in a single area—chart C13, which has no soundings but shows the main outer marks, treated in the following order. After these come the traverses between one main channel and another, followed by the inside channels. Finally, the harbours. A table of tidal currents is below.

1—la Croix from le Grand Chenal
2—la Croix from Chenal de la Moisie
3—la Croix from Chenal du Men-du-Castrec
4—la Croix from Chenal du Ferlas
5—la Croix from Chenal de Bréhat
6—Anse de Paimpol from Chenal de la Jument
7—Anse de Paimpol from Chenal SE de Ringue-Bras
8—Anse de Paimpol from Chenal de Plouézec
9—Anse de Paimpol from Chenal de Pors Moguer
10—Traverse, Men-du-Castrec to Bréhat
11—Traverse, Chenal du Ringue-Bras
12—River Trieux, Lézardrieux, Pontrieux
13—Traverse, Ferlas to Jument by Chenal du Denou
14—Traverse, Ferlas to Jument by Chenal St Rion
15—Traverse, Ferlas to Jument by Chenal de la Trinité
16—Traverse, Ferlas to Jument by Chenal du Lastel
17—Port Lazo
18—Paimpol
19—Porz Even
20—Ile de Bréhat, le Kerpont, Ile St Modé, Rade de Pommelin
21—l'Arcouest
22—Pen-ar-Ros
23—Loguivy

Place of reference—Héaux de Bréhat   Tidal Currents

	FLOOD			EBB		
	Direction	Spring Rate Knots	Starts at HW	Direction	Spring Rate Knots	Starts at HW
Anse de Paimpol N48°47′ W2°59′	SE	2·0	−6	NW	2·0	−1
Mez de Guelo N48°47′ W2°56′	SE	3·0	−6	NW	3·0	−1½
Cain-ar-Monse bouée N48°50′ W2°57′	S	4·0	−6	NNW	3·7	HW
Vieille de Tréou N48°52′ W3°01′	SW	3·2	−2	NE	3·2	+½
les Héaux N48°55′ W3°05′	E	2·6	−6	W	2·4	HW

The neap rates are about half the above spring rates; the times remain the same.

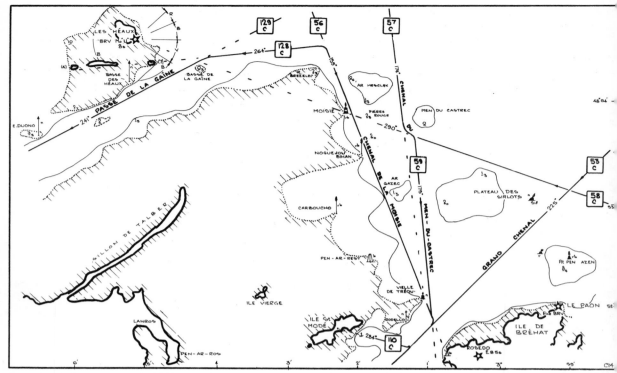

Chart C14—Entrée du Trieux

1—La Croix from Le Grand Chenal (11m)

The first five of the main channels are aimed to the entrance to the Pontrieux river, in fact they stop near la Vieille de Loguivy. It seems less cumbersome to call this crossroads by the name of the nearby light—la Croix. The river, by the way, is really named le Trieux though some charts use Pontrieux. See first charts C13 (p. 166) and C14 (above).

The channel is as easy by night as by day and the marks are the same,

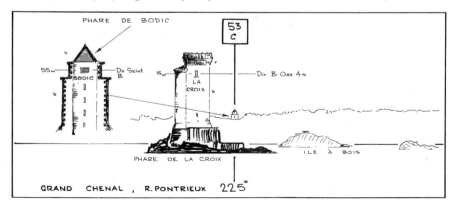

GRAND CHENAL, R. PONTRIEUX 225°

53C   Bodic light × la Croix light until 3–4 cables off the light,

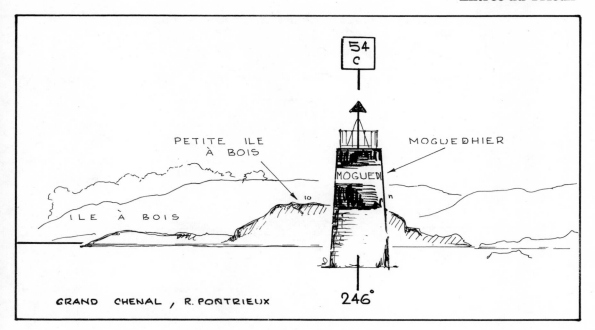

54C   Petite Ile à Bois × Moguedhier tourelle, see chart C15 (p. 172).

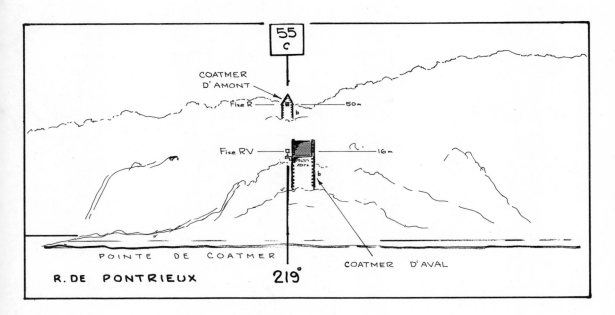

55C   the two Coatmer lights in line. The rest of the up-river part begins on p. 185.

2—La Croix from Chenal de la Moisie (6m)

This is the main approach from the NW or from Tréguier. If from the latter you would come east along the Passe de la Gaîne, included in the Tréguier marks.

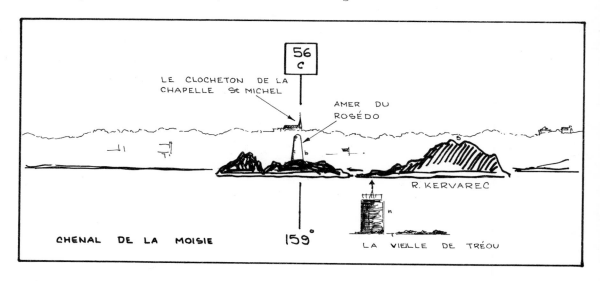

56C   St Michel's Chapelle × l'Amer du Rosédo. This must be carefully held as the line leaves Moisie tourelle (CE) only a few metres to stb'd, likewise Noguejou Bihan balise (CE) and later on Ar-Gazec *1·3m* 50m to port. When past Vieille de Tréou by 15m to stb'd join
53C   (225°) Grand Chenal (p. 168).

3—La Croix from Chenal du Men-du-Castrec (6m)

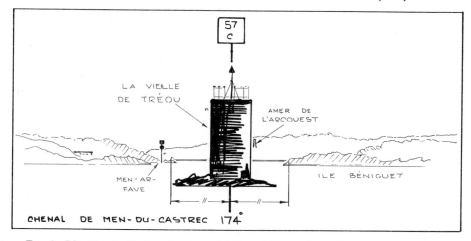

57C   Put la Vieille de Tréou in the middle of Chenal du Kerpont, which is the same as l'Amer de l'Arcouest but is more difficult to see. There is a small dog-leg to make to eastward when

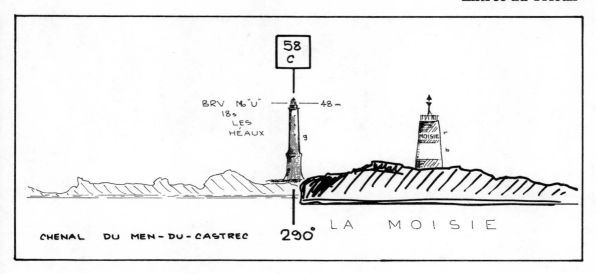

58C   les Héaux light well to the left of Moisie tourelle (CE) and after a mere cable

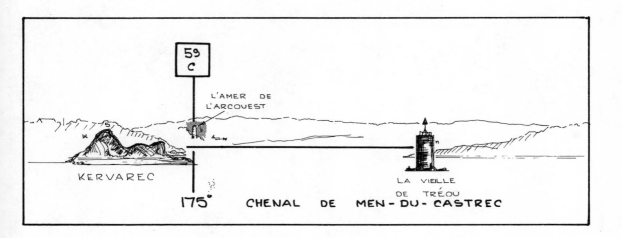

59C   l'Amer de l'Arcouest—nearer now— × Kervarec, a 5m high rock off Ile de Bréhat.
Again when past la Vieille de Tréou join
53C   (225°) Grand Chenal (p. 168).

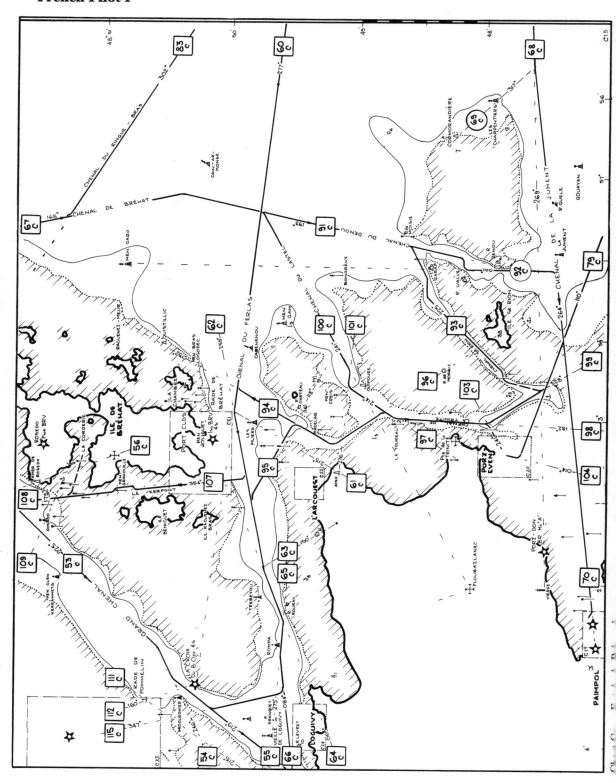

4—La Croix from Chenal du Ferlas (2·3m)

The whole of this is on chart C15 and it can be used at night as far as Men Joliguet light by keeping in the white sector.

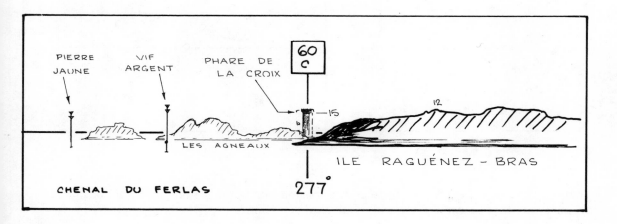

60C   la Croix light × left side of Ile Raguénez-Bras. This leaves Cain-ar-Monse (bouée CN) 4 cables to stb'd, and Cadenenou (bouée CN) ½ cable to port. When nearing les Piliers (tourelle CN) look for a breast mark,

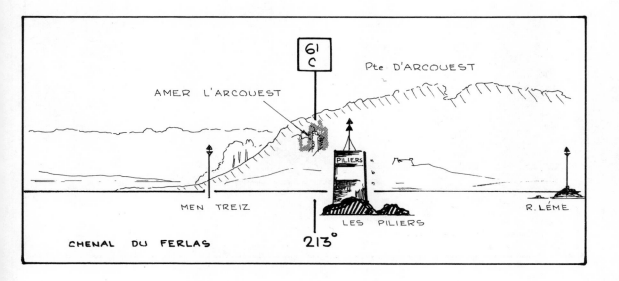

61C   l'Amer de l'Arcouest × les Piliers tourelle.

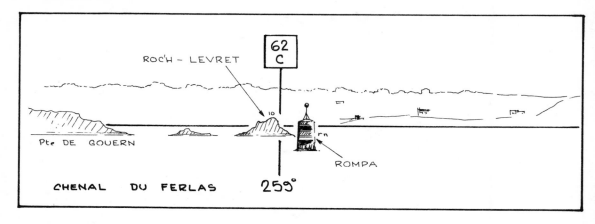

62C Roc'h Levret 10m high × Rompa tourelle (danger isolé) and after a mile and a quarter another breast mark, and a small change in course,

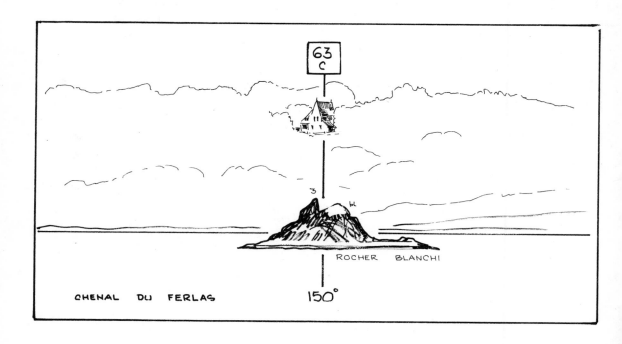

63C a prominent house × a whitened rock without a name. Then a stern mark

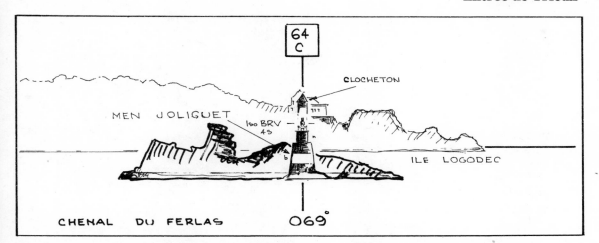

64C   the turret of a high house on Ile Logodec × Men Joliguet light.

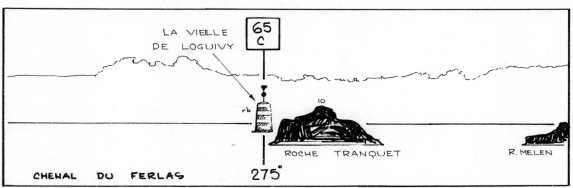

65C   la Vieille de Loguivy (tourelle bifurcation) × left side of Roche Tranquet, which leaves Rompa 50m to stb'd. Another stern mark

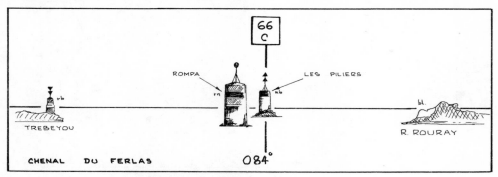

66C   les Piliers and Rompa in line, and so to join
55C   (219°) Grand Chenal (p. 169).
   There is a short cut here, to the east of Roche Tranquet, line 115C, on p. 203.

5—La Croix from Chenal de Bréhat (2·3m)

Use this channel when coming eastabout of Ile de Bréhat.

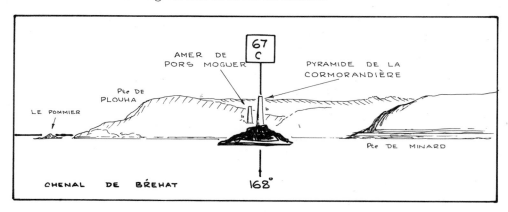

67C l'Amer de Pors Moguer × la Pyramide de la Cormorandière. Fair visibility is needed for this one—the back mark is 10 miles away when abreast of the north end of Ile de Bréhat. In fact, a glance at the chart shows that for 5–6 miles to the east of Ile de Bréhat there are vast areas of drying rocks. This and the following channels are safe ways through. Hold the mark until you join

60C (277°) Chenal du Ferlas (p. 173).

6—Anse de Paimpol from Chenal de la Jument (2·3m)

Anse de Paimpol is the anchorage south of Ile St Rion and the official pilotage mark is Paimpol New Church, N.D. de Bonne Nouvelle × Point Brividic but from a distance this is too vague. Instead here are two man-made marks. See chart C15 (p. 172).

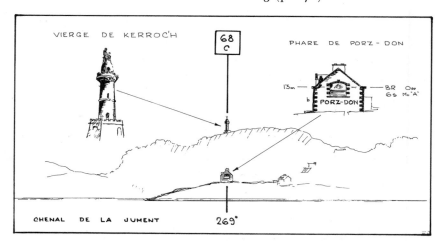

68C la Vierge de Kerroch × Porz-Don light. The back mark is distinctive. This is also the night route since the right limit of the white sector is the same bearing—269°. There is a breastmark for a slight change.

69C   (no view) la Cormorandière and les Charpentiers tourelles in line. From here onward use the same line, night or day,

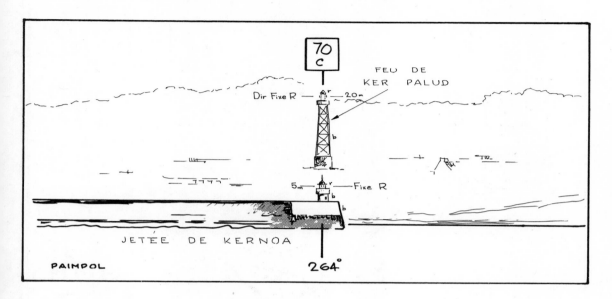

70C   Paimpol leading lights in line. This will take you right into Paimpol but for the moment we shall stop in the anchorage and resume later in section 18.

7—Anse de Paimpol from Chenal SE de Ringue-Bras (2·3m)
As the title suggests this clears all dangers coming in from the NE

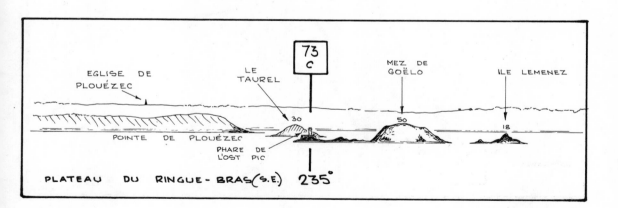

73C   le Taurel × l'Ost Pic light, which is also the night passage in the white sector of this light. It joins
68C   (269°) Chenal de la Jument (see opposite).

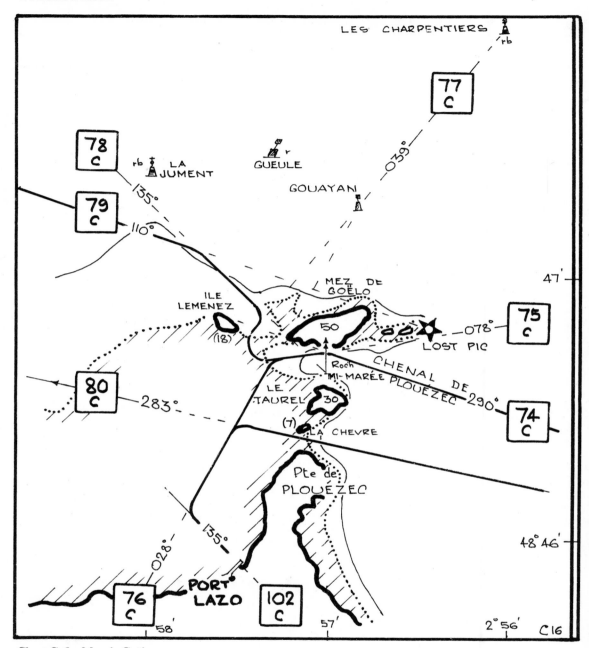

Chart C16—Mez de Goëlo

8—Anse de Paimpol from Chenal de Plouèzec (*2·om*)

An interesting backdoor entrance from the coast to the south, clear on chart C16. It avoids all the dangers east of l'Ost Pic.

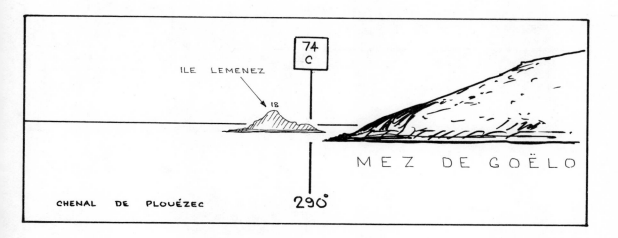

74C the right side of Ile Lemenez × the left side of Mez de Goëlo, until abreast of this mountain,

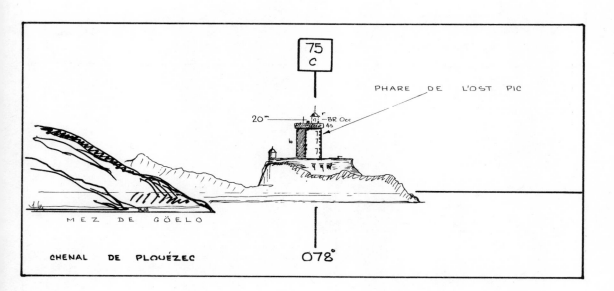

75C l'Ost Pic light well to the right of Mez de Goëlo, which leaves Roc'h Mi-Marée (balise CN) 100m to port. When Gouayan peeps round the corner of (76C)

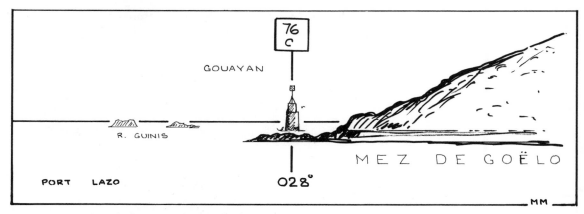

76C   Mez de Goëlo, come round to starboard until it is on with

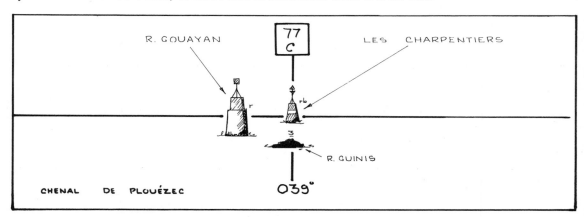

77C   les Charpentiers (tourelle CE) and stand by almost at once for a 90° port turn,

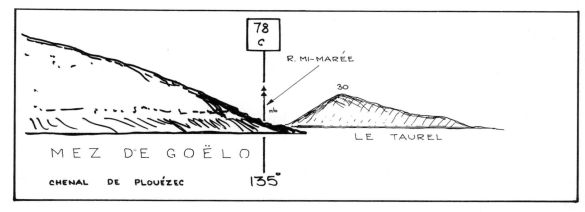

78C   Roc'h Mi-Marée balise × the right slope of Mez de Goëlo. After three cables take the final mark,

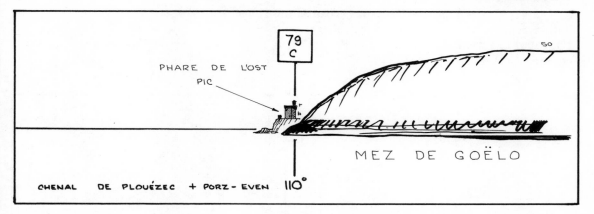

79C the light of l'Ost Pic just seen to the left of Mez de Goëlo, which leads across to the anchorage.

There is one alternative passage, south of la Chèvre,

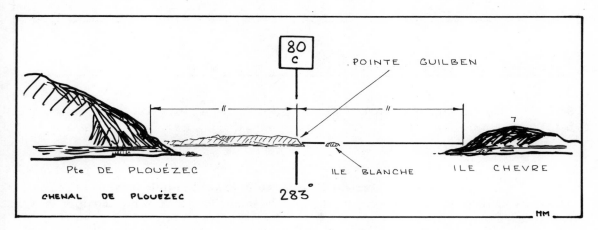

80C Pointe de Guilben halfway between Pointe de Plouèzec and la Chèvre. This dries $1 \cdot 2m$ in the centre.

9—Anse de Paimpol from Chenal de Pors Moguer (2·3m)

This is really the correct pilot mark to clear every single bank and rock east of la Horaine, Plateau du Men Marc'h, Plateau du Ringue-Bras, so therefore it is a tributary to the Jument channel.

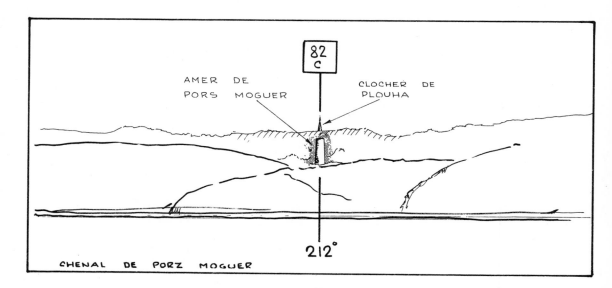

82C   Plouha Church × l'Amer de Pors Moguer. From this line you can peel off either using 60C (p. 173) or 68C (p. 176).

10—Traverse, Men-du-Castrec to Bréhat channels (5m)

This mark has been used in section 3; it was then the small dog-leg. Now it comes into its own so here it is again,

58C   les Héaux light well to the left of Moisie (tourelle CE (p. 171)). This traverse is two miles long, and cuts through the Grand Chenal also. See chart C14 (p. 168), and chart C13 (p. 166).

11—Traverse, Chenal du Ringue-Bras (7·1m)

Suppose you wish to sail south down the east of Ile de Bréhat, inside all those miles of rocks to seaward and then continue into the Baie de St Brieuc, then this is your route,

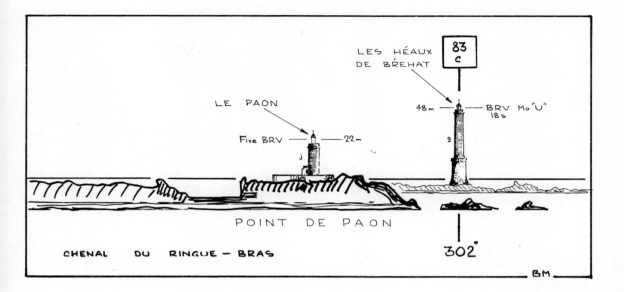

83C   les Héaux light well to the right (about 2 heights) of le Paon light. See chart C13 (p. 166).

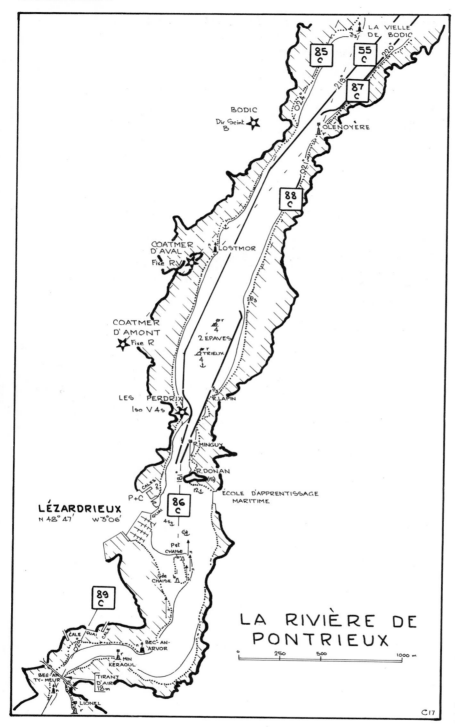

LA RIVIÈRE DE
PONTRIEUX

Chart C17—La
Rivière de Pontrieux

12—RIVER TRIEUX, LÉZARDRIEUX, PONTRIEUX

Here is where we take over from la Croix and go up river, quitting chart C15 (p. 172) and enjoying the trees and gorse of chart C17. This is delicate ground, being one of the Solent sailor's haunts and from time to time I see their yachting hats not at quite the correct angle. That's because they have run aground in an obviously deep and regular river. At springs there are one or two stones still not worn away during the last million years and the marks I'm going to give you are the official pilotage ones.

You are coming in on

55C   (219°) the two Coatmer lights in line (p. 169). When 300m past Olénoyère tourelle, take a stern mark.

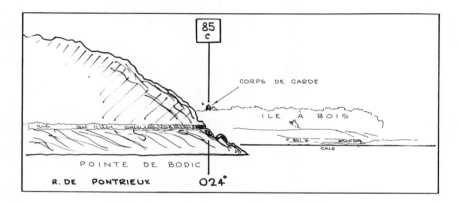

85C   the white watch-house on Ile à Bois × the high water mark of Pointe de Bodic. When abreast of the two wreck buoys—not to worry, there's 4m over both—look ahead,

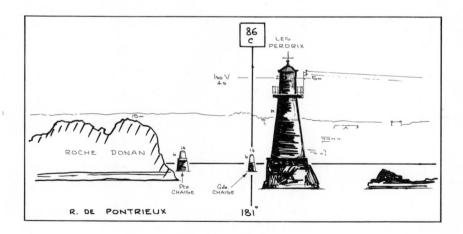

86C   the right hand of Grande Chaise tourelle × les Perdrix light. Leave the light 50m to stb'd. Now, and only now, can you take the middle of the river. There are a couple of marks downstream near Bodic, (87C)

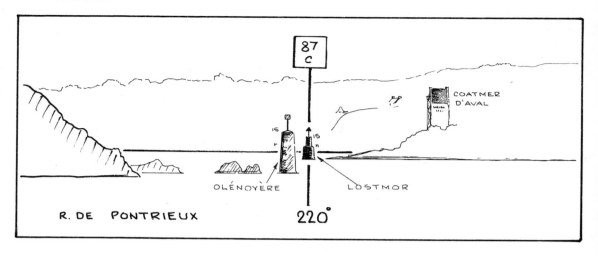

87C   Lostmor and Olénoyère tourelles in line clear the many rocks on the right bank near Loguivy—in case you are tacking upstream. To clear Roche Lapin, 3 heads, use

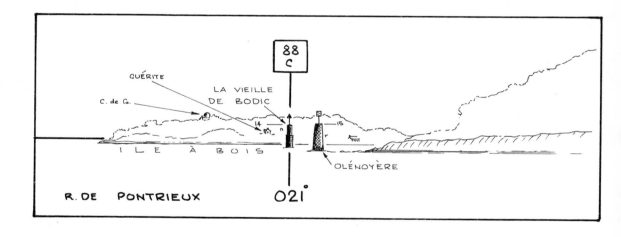

88C   la Vieille de Bodic just to the left of Olénoyère tourelle.

Lézardrieux, being one of the very few deep harbours, is crowded especially so with the new marina, which provides everything you could possibly want. It is only 500m to the village. Alternatively you may anchor or take one of the many buoys in the adjacent anchorage.

Have you ever been up river to Pontrieux? For a contrast to the cruel sea? If you can clear the bridge (a twin of Chelsea, it once carried a railway) on chart C17 (p. 184), no cables are lower elsewhere. It is about 3½ miles to Pontrieux and ships drawing 4·5m can make Pontrieux lock at springs, or 3·2m at neaps. It is normally open + and − one hour from HW which, at the lock, are the same times as St Malo.

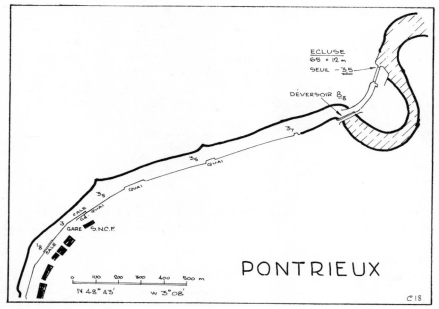

Chart C18—Pontrieux

Once through Lézardrieux bridge, take line

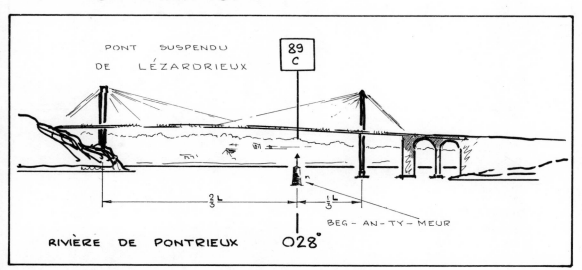

89C   Beg-an-Ty-Meur × the bridge piers as shown ($\frac{2}{3}$ and $\frac{1}{3}$ largeur) for a mile. But from there onwards you are on your own; mid-channel but always take the outside on bends. Chart C18 shows all, when you get there. The lock keepers are glad to see a stranger—a change from the sabliers. A Customs official is often in attendance—ask him for the key of the hot showers in passing. These, also clothes tubs, are on the quayside near the station.

French Pilot I

The best berths are between the 3·5m and 3·0m soundings; the rest of the right bank is for sabliers, etc. The town is 500m away but alongside there are cafés, a restaurant, the railway station. The place isn't geared to yachts, which is to be expected of a town still in the Middle Ages. Perhaps the Pontriviens—charming name—have forgotten that the French sacked the town twice, the English once. Yes, in 1345 by the Duke of Northampton! On the way down river stop a night at anchor by Roche Jagu, a 15th century fortified house, now a museum. There is a tunnel, dug by Richelieu down to the river, but it is quicker to climb through the woods.

I think it's time we slid seaward again, to learn some more channels.

13—Traverse, Ferlas to Jument by Chenal du Denou (2·8m)

There are several channels between Paimpol and Bréhat, this one starts from 60C, see chart C15 (p. 172).

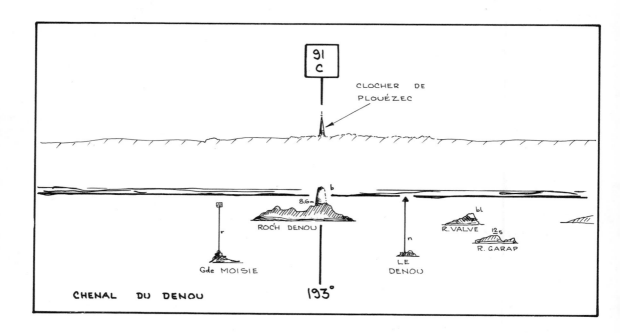

91C   Plouézec Church × Roc'h Denou (tourelle blanche) which passes through a gateway, Grande Moisie (port balise) and le Denou (stb'd balise). When past the latter by 3 cables, i.e. abreast of a whitened rock, Roc'h Valve, steer so as to leave Roc'h Denou (8·6m high, with tourelle) 20m to port but on a course

92C   (no view) of 181° out into the Chenal de la Jument. This last line is, in fact, a transit of Men Garo tourelle (CE) × the summit of Garap *12·5m.*

14—Traverse, Ferlas to Jument by Chenal St Rion (*0·0m*)

This one is a bit sparse on marks but is the most frequently used channel by the Paimpol trawlers, one of whose skippers taught me the passage. It is best taken below half tide so that the marginal rocks are showing. Coming south along line 91C, branch off when abreast of Grande Moisie balise and keep it on a stern bearing 067° for 2 cables only, until abreast of Garap *12·5m* when immediately come onto line

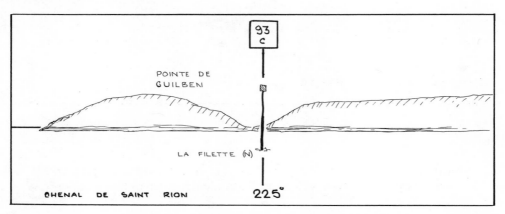

93C   la Fillette—the most northerly of two balises—in a notch on Pointe de Guilben. You are now in a mile long 'river' with rocks on both sides. Leave the above balise 25m to port and steer out into the Chenal de la Jument.

15—Traverse, Ferlas to Jument by Chenal de la Trinité (*0·0m*)

This is most frequently used between Paimpol and Bréhat, is nearest the shore and has firm transits all the way. There are two entrances from the north, but coming from line 60C (p. 173),

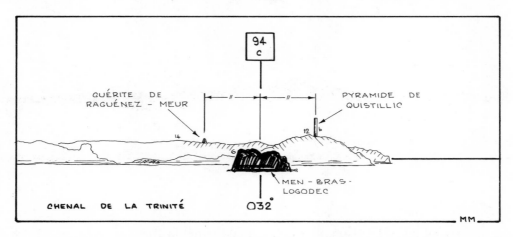

94C   Men-Bras-Logodec midway between the watch house on Raguénez-Meur (an islet east of Bréhat) and Quistillic tourelle. A bit of a mouthful but clear marks. The western entrance is as long-winded, (95C)

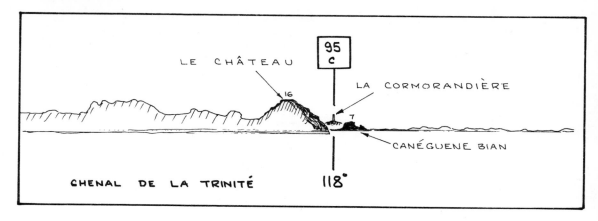

95C   tourelle de la Cormorandière midway between Canéguene-Bian and le Château (highest rock hereabouts). Both marks join until after leaving la Madeline balise (CW) a cable to port,

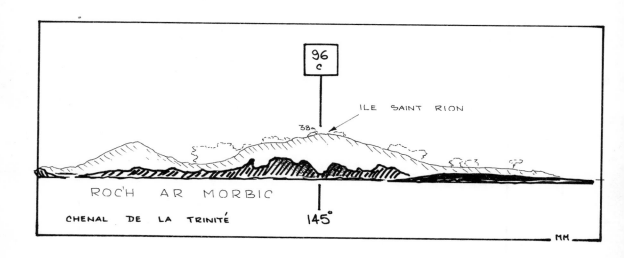

96C   the summit of Ile Rion × a well-defined notch in Roc'h-ar-Morbic. This line is over a sandbank, the shallowest part of the Chenal *o·om*, which would otherwise carry 2m throughout. To avoid a small rock a cable north of le Toureau we have to use a Chenal du Lastel mark, but an easy one,

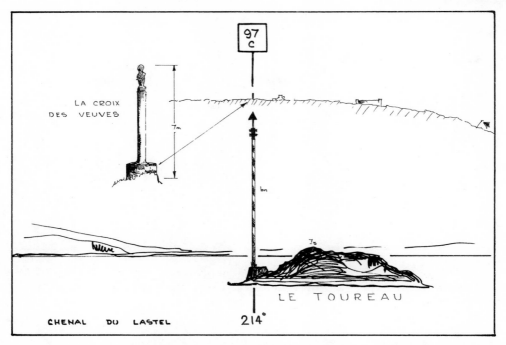

97C   la Croix des Veuves × le Toureau (balise transition). This is where fishermens' wives waited for their men to return from Iceland each season; after 3–4 weeks there could be but one conclusion—a black dress.

However, having left that most decorative balise, le Toureau 6om to stb'd,

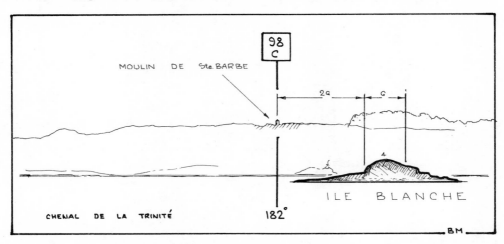

98C   the old windmill of Ste. Barbe × the left of Ile Blanche—twice its high water width. This leaves Rollic balise 50m to stb'd, Min Treuze 7om to port, Queroie 100m to port, Clividy (balise bifurcation) 100m to stb'd, but just before coming abreast of this last balise, take a stern mark, (99C)

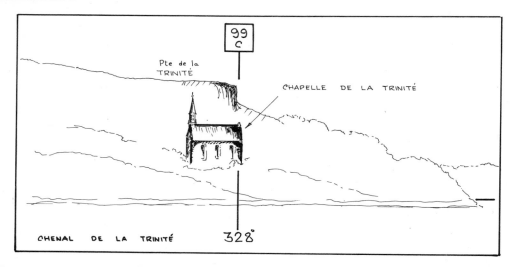

99C   the cliff behind Chapelle de la Trinité × the right end of its roof, which takes you right out into the Chenal de la Jument. Incidentally, here, just where 99C and 98C intersect, is an excellent anchorage in about 3m, sand and mud. Another, even better, is where 99C meets 79C in 7m, mud and gravel.

16—Traverse, Ferlas to Jument by Chenal du Lastel (1·6m)

Here is a tributary to the Trinité channel, but deeper and slightly easier. Start where the Denou joins Chenal du Ferlas,

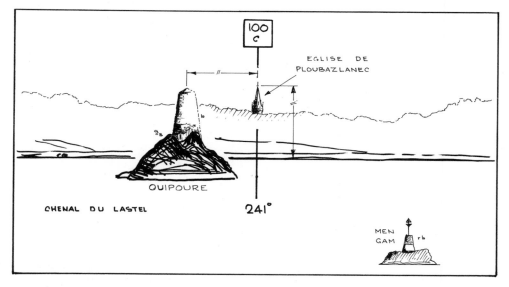

100C   Ploubazlanec Church to the right of Ouipoure by its height, which leaves Men Gam (CE) $2\frac{1}{2}$ cables to stb'd. When 2 cables off the white tourelle steer westish.

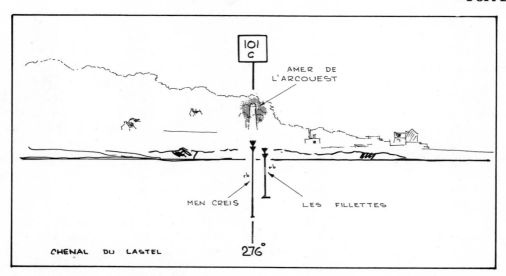

101C   les Fillettes × Men Creis, the only two CS balises here, then immediately turn to port to take the previous line

97C   (214°) la Croix des Veuves × that maypole balise, le Toureau (p. 191). From here onward it is the Chenal de la Trinité.

17—PORT LAZO

Hardly worth considering, but I once had need of it one night when the whole of the Paimpol estuary was white over from a sudden SE gale.

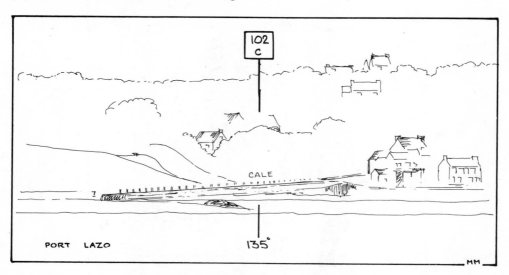

102C   shows all there is, a long slip with a km walk for bread. As you can see from chart C16 (p. 178), 76C is an approach line on account of some old oyster beds inshore.

18—PAIMPOL

From the Anse de Paimpol to the town, 70C, the two leading light structures are clearly visible, but there are 10 stb'd balises and buoys and 4 to port. Chart C19 details this fine port and wet basin; a relic of the Iceland cod fleets of the last century or so.

The lock functions about + and − 1½ hours HW, but often waits for a collection of boats. Both gates are left open + and − one hour if the rise in tide at les Héaux exceeds 8m. If less than that, the time is cut to + and − 30 minutes only. They operate day and night. Good drying berths are alongside Jetée de Kernoa or in the small Port d'Echouage. Note the two lock cills are of different heights.

Once through the gates the Port de Plaisance is directly ahead—hot showers, chandlery, two sailmakers, three boatbuilders, cranes and a slipway. Railway station with trains to the Brest–Paris line via Guingamp. The famous Iles Glénan Sailing School has a branch here. Beauport Abbey is 2½km walk on the south of the estuary.

Pierre Loti's classic 'Pêcheurs d'Islande' tells of some 80 goelettes sailing for the north; whose crews 'not until they retired did they see the spring flowers'. It would be poor taste to remind the kind Paimpolais that it was one of their citizens Capt. Gersale, who shot Nelson at Trafalgar.

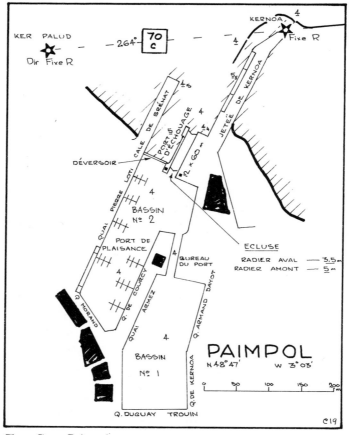

Chart C19—Paimpol

19—PORZ-EVEN

A dozen or so chalutiers fish out of this sheltered but drying harbour. There are two entrances, the first from the Trinité channel, chart C20,

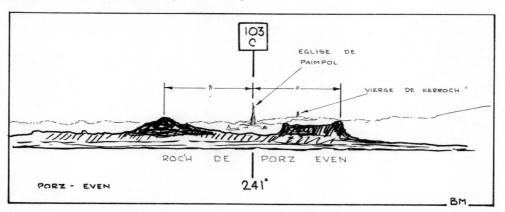

103C   Paimpol Church between the two heads of Roc'h de Porz-Even, but this one dries *3·5m*.

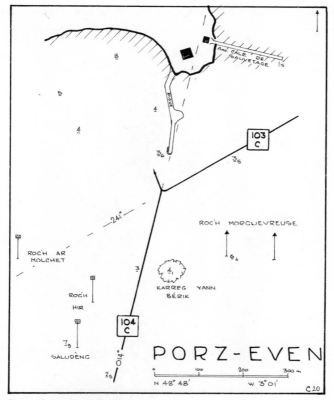

Chart C20—Porz-Even

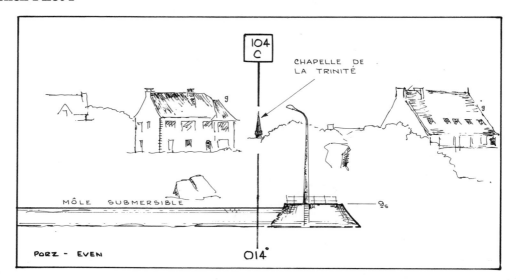

104C   is better, Chapelle de la Trinité × the lamp post on the end of the quay. The mole covers at springs, about a metre. The fishing boats lie up to half a mile to the south, where they can stay afloat longer, so there are clear drying berths anywhere west of the mole. Its sides slope so you can't lie alongside. There are shops, a café and a restaurant within 500m.

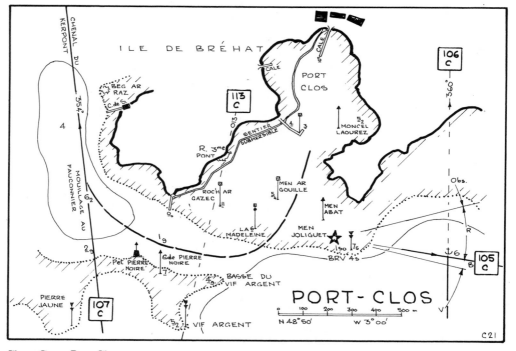

Chart C21—Port-Clos

20—ILE DE BRÉHAT, LE KERPONT, ILE ST MODÉ, RADE DE POMMELIN

Ile de Bréhat and my home, Sark, are almost twins. The population, size, vegetation, ecology (no cars) is the same. Also, unfortunately, the number of grockles who invade each season amounts to the identical figure. But Bréhat has four wonderful anchorages, la Chambre to the east, Port-Clos at the south, Kerpont and la Corderie to the west.

La Chambre is on chart C15 (p. 172) and it requires no marks; simply keep between the balises and pick a clear spot. The bottom is sand and gradually shoals to 6·5m opposite a slip on Bréhat.

The ferry harbour for goods and passengers is Port-Clos on chart C21, a simple entrance from the south. The many ferries shuttle between here and l'Arcouest, but the goods come from Paimpol through the Trinité channel. Stay afloat either south of Men Joliguet or take a tideless anchorage just to the east, or dry out anywhere inside. An excellent anchorage is,

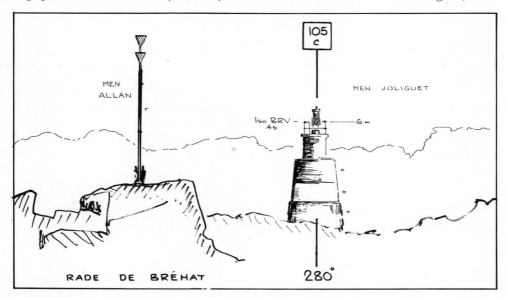

105C   Men Joliguet light × Men Allan balise, and put this in line with

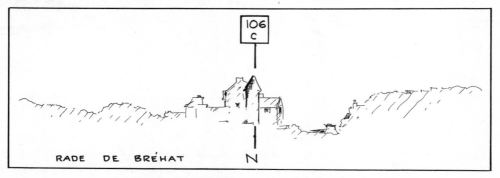

106C   a turreted house due north, in about 6m sand and gravel.

Use le Chenal du Kerpont to carry on round to the west side but north of chart C21 it starts to dry 1·5m but on line (107C)

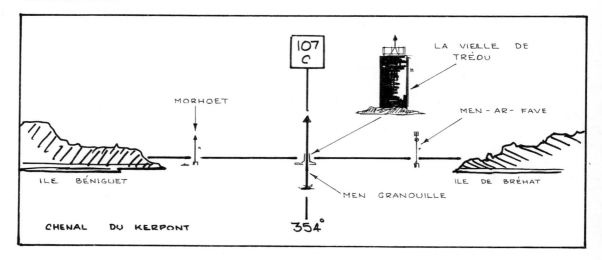

107C   la Vieille de Tréou tourelle × Men Granouille, which is the mark for le Kerpont, there is another fine anchorage. This is Mouillage au Fauconnier in 6·2m near the lifeboat slip where there is also a painted rock, Beg-ar-Raz. Strong tide, but good holding.

Continuing north up the Kerpont, leave Men Granouille to port by 10m, then use it as a stern mark, see chart C15 (p. 172).

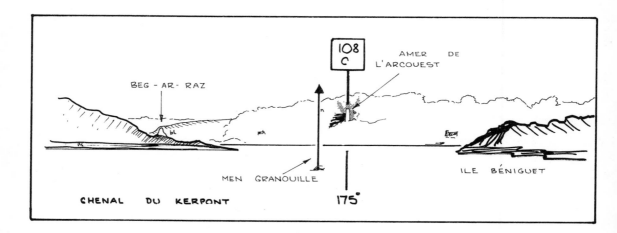

108C   Men Granouille × l'Amer de l'Arcouest which after a mile joins the Grand Chenal, line 53C (p. 168). The route into la Corderie is shown on chart C15 (p. 172), balises both sides of the entrance. The anchorage dries up to 6·7m but is of use at neaps. Land at the slip, shown on the north side. All provisions can be bought in Bréhat in the village, le Bourg.

There is a small deep anchorage out of the tide just north of Kervarec, the rock pictured in view 59C (p. 171), the marks are

198

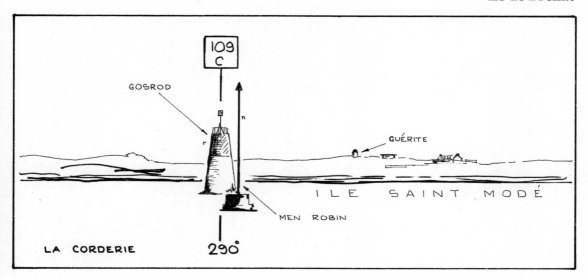

109C Gosrod tourelle × Men Robin balise. Go as far in as the tide allows. A few locals keep their boats here.

Though a private island, Ile St Modé offers a tideless anchorage, line

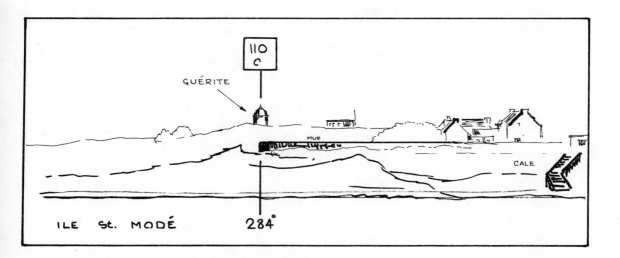

110C the watch-house × the left end of a seawall—chart C14 (p. 168); a couple of cables off the slip there is 2m, mud and sand.

The last anchorage to know about—though there are many more—is for ships, la Rade de Pommelin. A few cables NW of la Croix light in 7m to 9m, mud and shells. The two marks are,

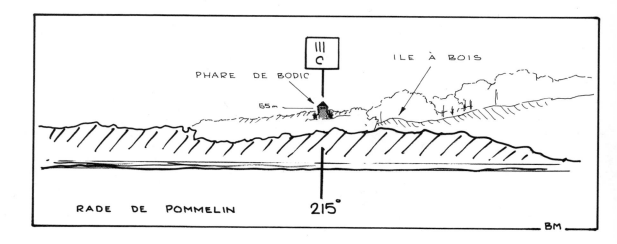

111C   Bodic light × the left side of Ile à Bois (if you can see the wood for the trees) and,

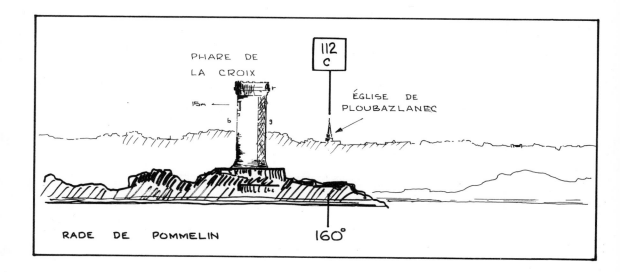

112C   Ploubazlanec Church × la Croix light. Two hundred years ago coasters anchored here under the watchful eyes of the Douane, whose house remains a mile upstream on Roc'h-ar-On. The nearby tourelle, Olénoyère (salt gatherer) may refer to the ancient tax on their commodity.

21—L'ARCOUEST

This is merely a ferry terminal and the long slip is on chart C22. There is a café ashore however, but a long walk to Ploubazlanec, the nearest village. The ferry skippers use a mark in Bréhat,

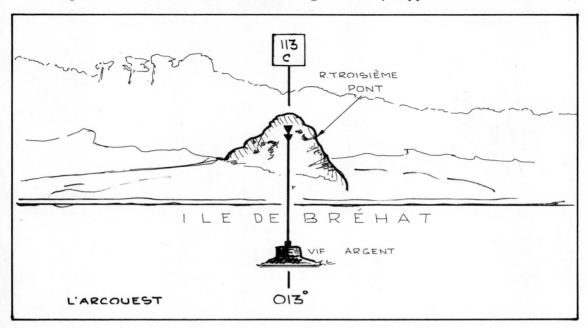

113C   Roc'h de la Troisième Pont (what a name!) × le Vif Argent (balise CS).

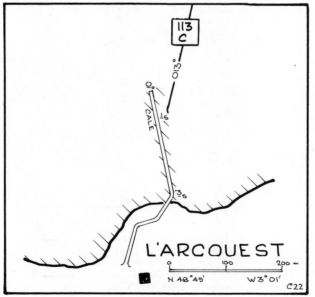

Chart C22—L'Arcouest

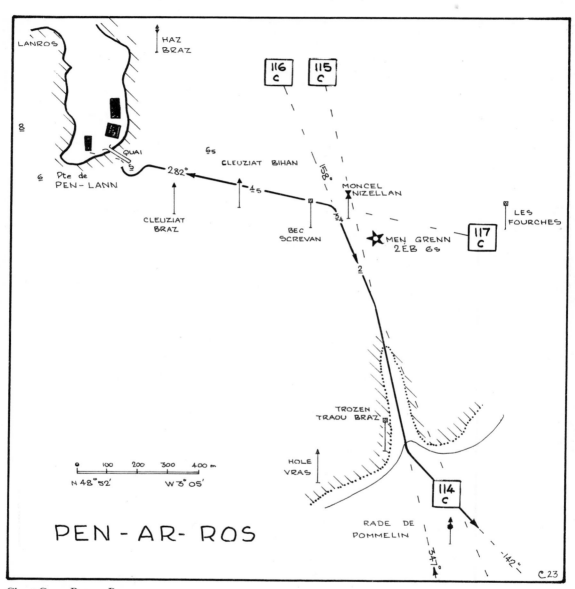

Chart C23—Pen-ar-Ros

22—PEN-AR-ROS

Here is a forgotten harbour of vanished importance, but still well marked, shown on chart C23. The route starts off at the Rade de Pommelin

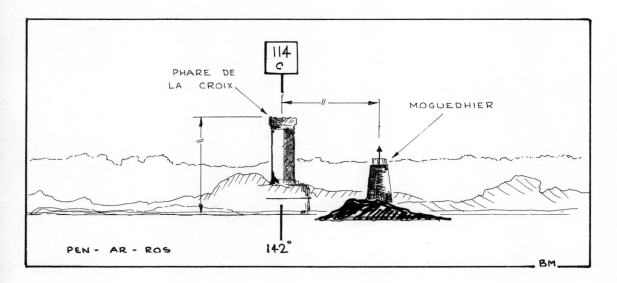

114C la Croix light its height to the left of Moguedhier tourelle. Just before reaching Trozen Traou Braz balise take

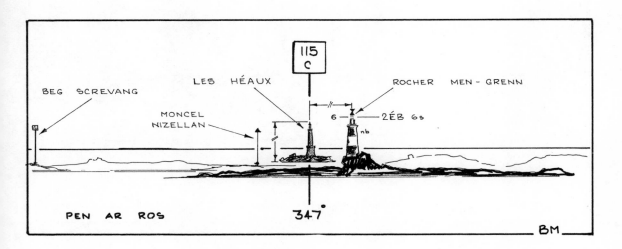

115C les Héaux light 4 miles away, its height to the left of Men-Grenn light. I've never worked out the reason for this light, surely not for this unused channel? A cable before the light take (116C)

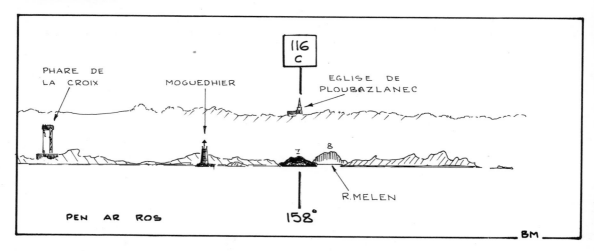

116C   Ploubazlanec Church × an unnamed rock *7·om*. The rock is distinctive and close, in the view, to a monster, Roc'h Melen. This takes you through a gateway of two balises until the entrance mark comes,

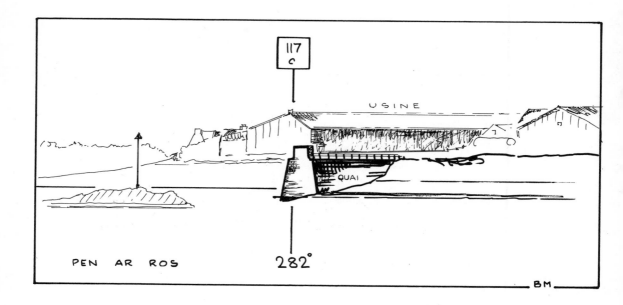

117C   the end of a long shed × the end of the quay. The berth alongside the south of the miniature quay dries *5m* at the end, *7m* at the head.

23—LOGUIVY

Chart C24 details this fishing port where a dozen or so boats lie to deep moorings just outside. The entrance line clears the various viviers,

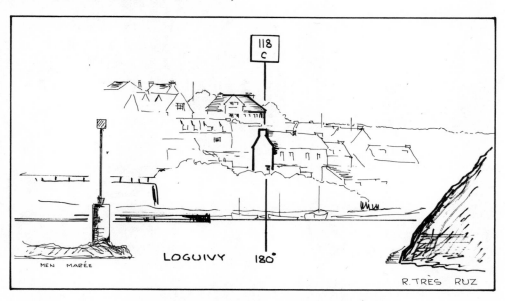

118C two houses in line. There is ample room inside to dry out but not alongside. The amenities are that of a fishing village.

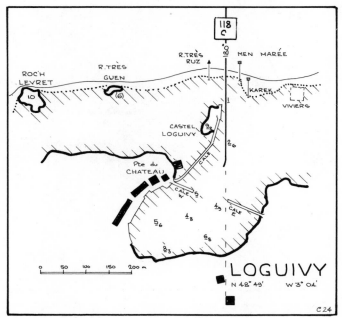

Chart C24—Loguivy

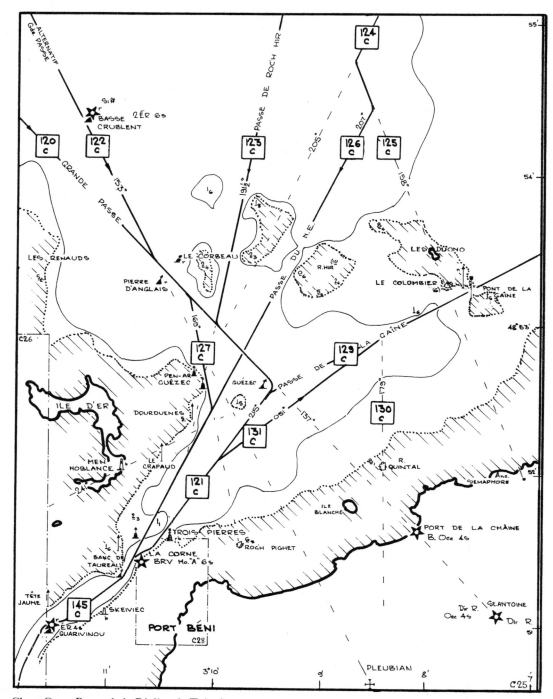

Chart C25—Passes de la Rivière de Tréguier

TRÉGUIER RIVER

Only 40 miles from Guernsey and an easy entrance day or night makes the deep river of Tréguier a favourite north Brittany refuge. It is worth a visit if only to see the fine old borough, the birthplace of France's only honest lawyer, St Yves. The town's patron saint—also that of all advocates, and of the poor (significant combination)—was born in 1255. An oratory to his memory is at Port Blanc.

The tide in the approach channels is about the same as that near les Héaux lighthouse, in the table on p. 167. In the river the current is regular and reaches 2½ knots at springs on the flood and ebb, near la Corne light. Slack is at LW and HW; neap rate about half. See chart C25.

The Tréguier area is divided thus:

> 1—Grande Passe with an alternative
> 2—Passe de Roc'h Hir
> 3—Passe du Nord Est
> 4—Passe de la Gaine
> 5—Chenal de Men-Dall
> 6—Chenal du Château
> 7—Tréguier
> 8—Port Béni

Channels 1–6 above terminate on the river mouth in the area about north of la Corne.

1—Grande Passe (4·4m)

The same marks are used by night as by day,

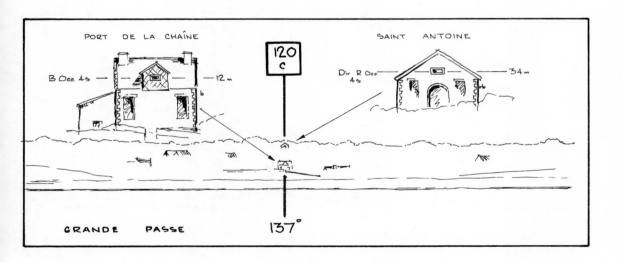

120C   St Antoine × Port de la Chaîne lights, which line leads between le Corbeau (port) and Pierre d'Anglais (stb'd) buoys, then round the Guézec stb'd buoy by 100m,

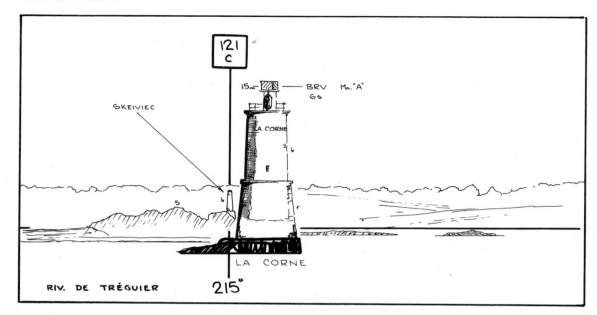

121C Skeivic tourelle × left of la Corne light, or at night in the white sector of this light. The remainder of the river is in section 7. There is one practical snag with line 120C in that it is difficult to pick out the two small buildings which serve as lighthouses. The front light can be mistaken for other similar buildings and the rear one shyly pokes out of a wood. So may I recommend as a long distance mark line

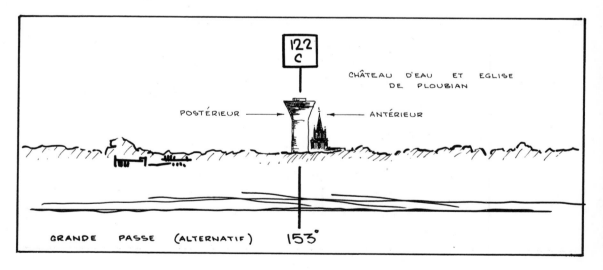

122C the water-tower exactly touching Ploubian Church. Almost no daylight should show between them, a simple matter since both are on the skyline. This line joins 121C in the gateway just mentioned.

208

2—Passe de Roc'h Hir (2·2m)

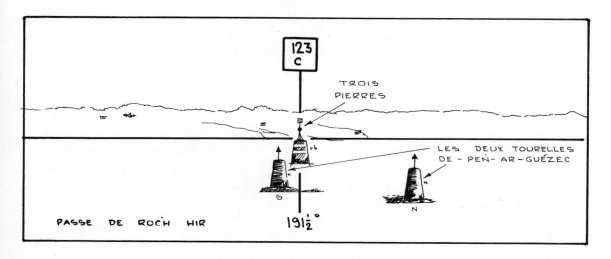

123C Les Trois Pierres (tourelle bifurcation) × the tourelle sud de Pen-ar-Guézec
which joins
120C (137°) Grande Passe (p. 207).

3—Passe du Nord Est (2·6m)
In spite of the dog-leg this is a much used channel coming from the NE

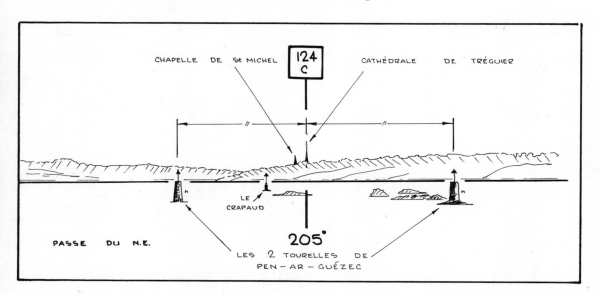

124C Cathédrale de Tréguier (the right hand spire of two) midway between the two
Pen-ar-Guézec tourelles. The breast mark for the zig-zag is (125C)

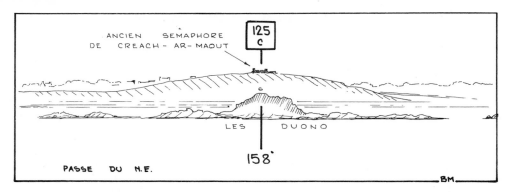

125C   the old semaphore on Creach-ar-Maout × the highest rock in les Duono 6m high. The line is less than 4 cables long, before

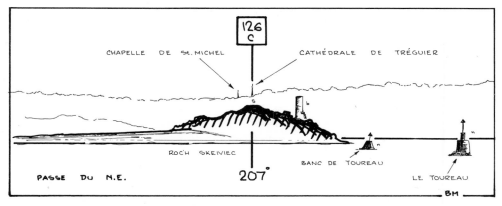

126C   Tréguier Cathédral again × the summit of Roc'h Skeiviec which leads right down to la Corne, crossing 120C en route.

A short cut inside the *1·5m* patch, Guézec is line

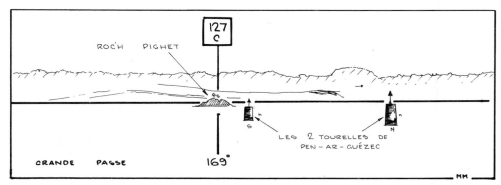

127C   Roc'h Pighet, prominent on the shore × the left of the tourelle sud de Pen-ar-Guézec, which joins

126C   (207°) Passe du Nord Est (see above).

4—Passe de la Gaîne (0·3m)

The traditional route coastwise from the River Trieux to Tréguier, but you must be able to see 7 miles. Even so, in the evening light it is a hard job to find the back mark. The best route if you are coming from Bréhat is to return to chart C14 (p. 168) and sail north up the Chenal de la Moisie 56C until

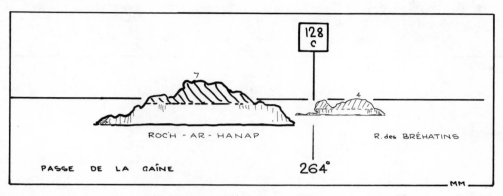

128C left side of Roc'h des Bréhatins × right side of Roc'h-ar-Hanap. Both are prominent rocks in the Héaux group. After a mile on this mark, which is to clear north of Basse de la Gaîne *0·3m* find

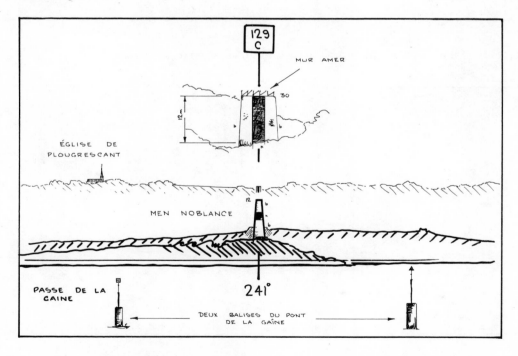

129C l'Amer de Plougrescant × Men Noblance tourelle. The far mark is only just clear of trees; the odd-shaped top is the remains of an effort to make it more visible. It is a row of

angled reflectors which I fancy didn't last out their first gale. From chart C14 (p. 168) it will be seen that you must keep dead on the marks to avoid a *2·om* rock. The line leaves two stb'd balises a bare cable off before coming on to chart C25 (p. 206). At Pont de la Gaîne there is a 150m wide gateway between two balises, and this is useful because if that amer is invisible, and it's still nearly 5 miles away, merely put Men Noblance in this gateway. Once past the Pont de la Gaîne watch out for the Basse du Colombier *1·6m* only 30m north of the marks. There is a breast mark now for a slight change,

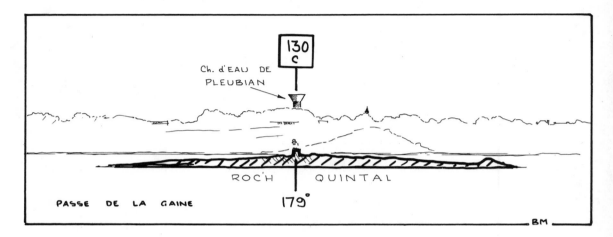

130C   Pleubian water-tower × Roc'h Quintal, then a stern mark

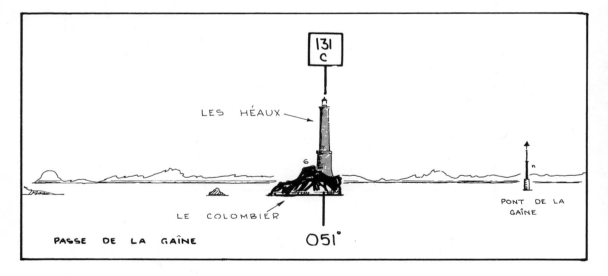

131C   les Héaux light × le Colombier which joins
121C   (215°) Grande Passe (p. 208).

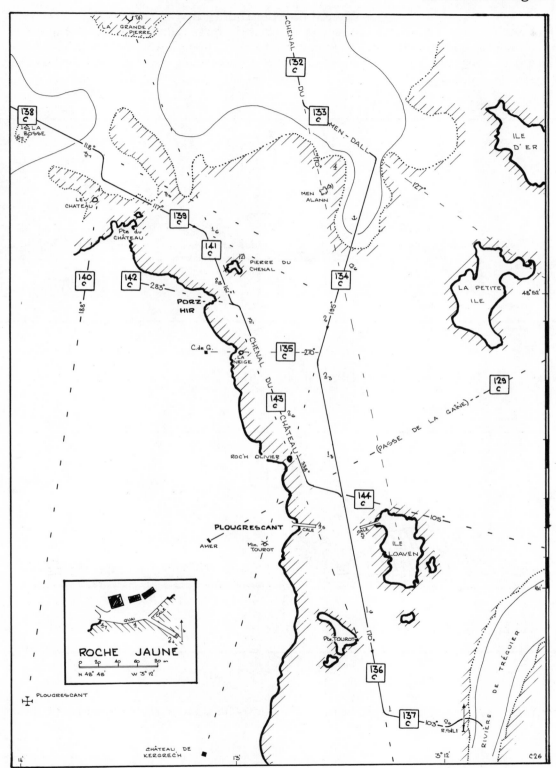

Chart C26—Chenaux du Men-Dall et du Château

5—Chenal du Men-Dall (*3·1m*)

This and the next one are interesting channels but since the right rise of tide is important I would suggest good weather and no hurry. That is why I have always used them for leaving Tréguier rather than entering. Half tide, equal to a rise of about 5·5m, is about the best time. See chart C26 (p. 213).

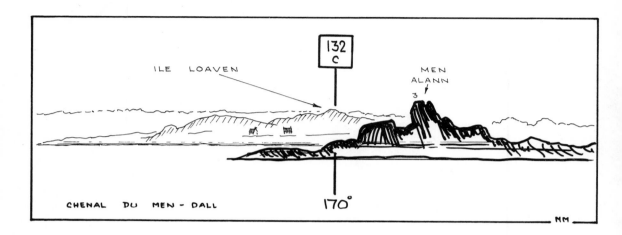

132C   Ile Loaven summit × the left side of Men Alann, about 3·0m high.

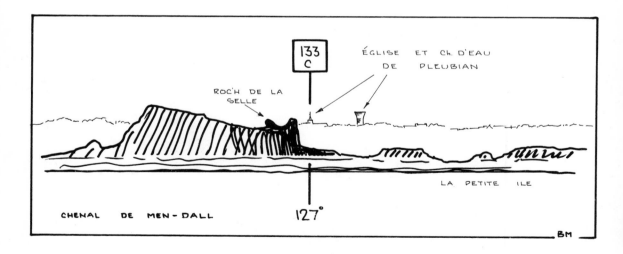

133C   Pleubian Church × the right of a saddle-shaped rock at the north of la Petite Ile.

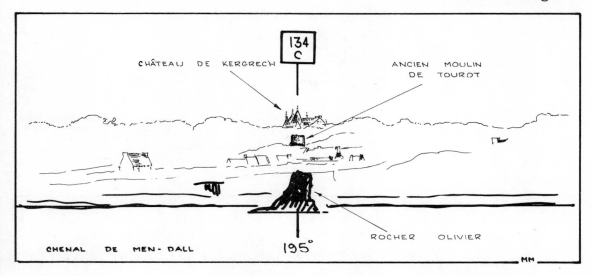

CHÂTEAU DE KERGREC'H | 134 C | ANCIEN MOULIN DE TOUROT

ROCHER OLIVIER

CHENAL DE MEN-DALL — 195°

134C   What luck, three marks! Château de Kergrec'h × the old windmill Tourot × Rocher Olivier. Until this transit started there has up till now been 10m of water. So if there isn't enough depth, here is the place to anchor in shelter; on this line 134C and east of Men Alann. A breast mark now, a bit before the actual turn

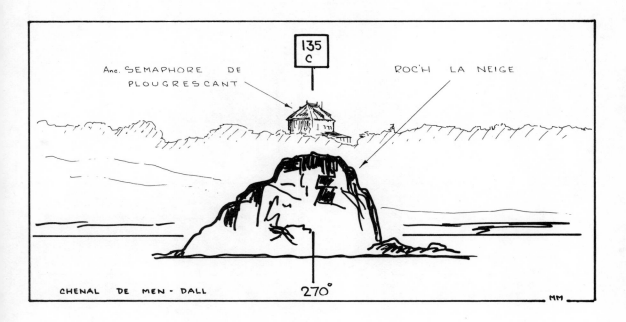

Anc. SEMAPHORE DE PLOUGRESCANT | 135 C | ROC'H LA NEIGE

CHENAL DE MEN-DALL — 270°

135C   the old semaphore × Roc'h la Neige, on the shore.

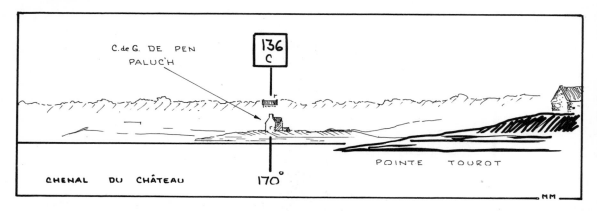

136C　　a mile long mark, a house across the river × the old coast-guard on Pen Paluc'h. This passes between two slips. One on the mainland and the other on Ile Loaven. Not a bad place to dry out, try the Plougrescant side, about the 'L' of cale. If not, carry on until the turn into the river.

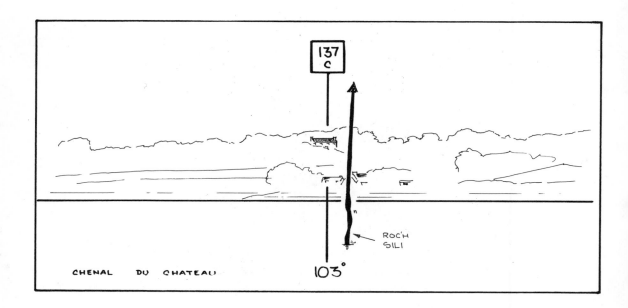

137C　　a farmhouse across the river × Roc'h Sili balise.

6—Chenal du Château (*4·5m*)

This has a clearer entrance than the last channel but dries more. However, it is the only route from the river to a small harbour, Porz Hir. The first two marks are on one view

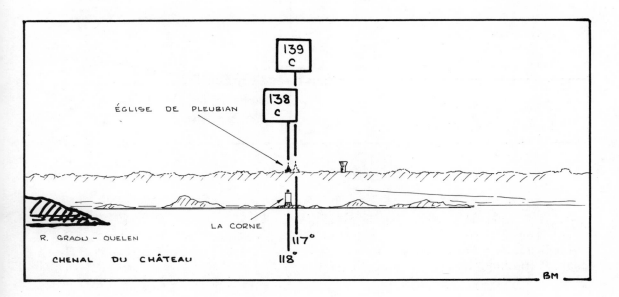

138C   Pleubian Church × la Corne light exactly, until a breast mark for a small zig-zag

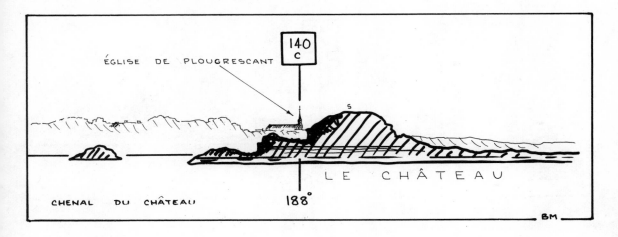

140C   Plougrescant Church × a large rock, le Château, 5·0m high. After a stb'd dog-leg of a cable, look again at the previous view for

139C   the same church but this time open to the right of la Corne light by its diameter, exactly as drawn (see above).

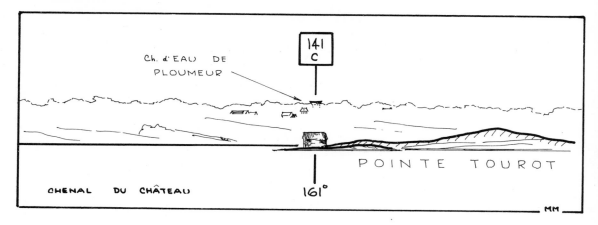

CHENAL DU CHÂTEAU

141C   the water-tower, only just visible above trees, in Ploumeur ✕ a granite hut on Pointe Tourot. Sorry about the low water-tower but it is only for a couple of cables, to take you through a stone gateway. To port, Pierre du Chenal, 2m high. To stb'd, Roc'h de Porz Hir, 7m high. Peep round this last mountain for

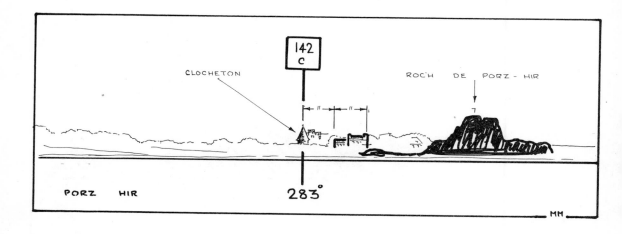

PORZ HIR

142C   the turret of a villa to the left of a pair of houses on the beach, by their width. These are the Porz Hir entrance marks, several boats are kept here and the bottom is smooth sand for drying out. But this is also the breast mark for a small joggle eastward to a stern transit.

218

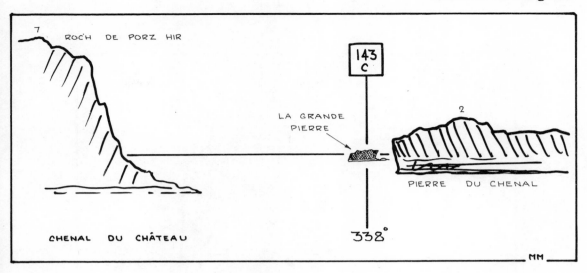

143C   la Grande Pierre, a mile out to sea, × the left face of Pierre du Chenal. Hold this course for half a mile for the third and last zig-zag,

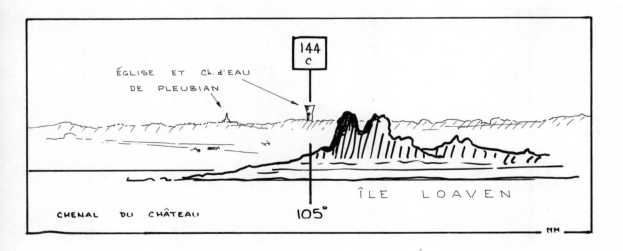

144C   Pleubian water-tower × the most northerly rock of Ile Loaven, which joins
136C   (170°) Chenal du Men-Dall (p. 216).

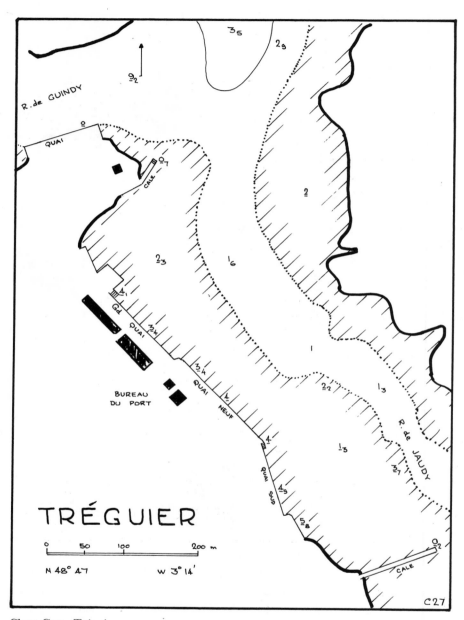

R. de GUINDY

QUAI

CALE

2₃

Gd
QUAI

BUREAU
DU PORT

QUAI NEUF

QUAI SUD

CALE

2

1₆

2₂

1₃

1₃

R. de JAUDY

TRÉGUIER

0	50	100	200 m

N 48° 47   W 3° 14'

C 27

Chart C27—Tréguier

7—TRÉGUIER

The route from just north of la Corne, where the various major channels congregate is simple and the minimum depth is 5m as far as Roche Jaune. So back to chart C25 (p. 206) and to avoid the bank NW of Trois Pierres, take

121C   Skeiviec tourelle just to the left of la Corne light (p. 208). This leaves les Trois Pierres (tourelle bifurcation) 100m to port. When past, steer to leave la Corne 75m to port (this is actually on line 126C but it is unimportant) and Banc du Taureau (bouée noire) 25m to stb'd then a stern mark.

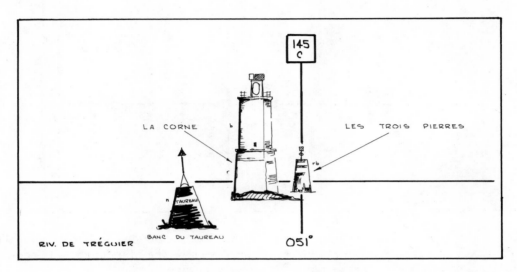

145C   les Trois Pierres tourelle × right of la Corne light. Next leave Guarivinou (bouée rouge) a few metres to port. The remainder of the four miles of very pleasant river up to Tréguier is well buoyed or posted. The port buoys are numbered 4, 6, 8, 10, 12, the starboard 1, 3, 5, 7, 9, 11. There are so many river anchorages that it is hardly worth listing them. There is one almost out of the current about a cable upstream of buoy '3' as close in to the left bank as the tide will allow.

Half a mile above buoy '4' there is a quay and slip—an oyster and fishing harbour—Roche Jaune. A thumbnail plan is on chart C26 (p. 213). A good drying berth is alongside the *4·0m* quay in hard sand and oyster shells. A dozen fishing boats are moored in the stream opposite.

Chart C27 shows the anchorage in Tréguier and the quays. If you care to lie alongside, which is preferable to the crowded anchorage, there are 400m of mostly empty quays at your disposal. Several moorings have been laid by the town authorities, if you care to trust these. I don't, but there is usually plenty of anchoring room. The port is at the confluence of the rivers Guindy and Jaudy, the resultant being the Tréguier. There are three bridges not shown on chart C27:

Pont Canada over the Jaudy, headway . . . 11·2m
Road bridge over the Guindy, headway . . . 13·2m
Foot bridge over the Guindy, headway . . . 11·2m
One day perhaps I'll discover where these two inviting rivers lead to.

There are showers at the yacht club, water on the quays, a magnificent cathedral of the 13th century, and all the beauty of an ancient town of some 4000 Bretons.

8—PORT BÉNI

A rather nondescript harbour but one to lie in alongside and in solitary splendour. The entrance is from the north, just to the east of les Trois Pierres balise, see chart C28. First pass between the gateway formed by Notar balise and the balise of les Trois Pierres, then a slight dog-leg to port on

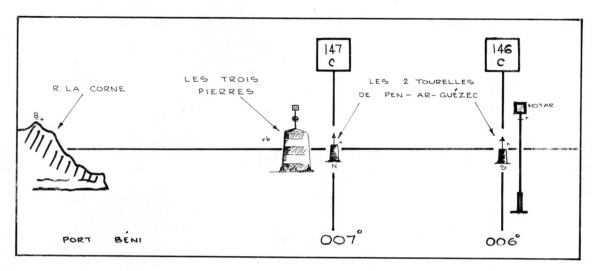

146C   a stern mark, the right of the two Pen-ar-Gúezec tourelles × Notar balise. This and the next mark are on the same view, so when 50m off Roche Marchande balise dog-leg again, this time to stb'd passing the balise 25m to port, on line

147C   the left of the two Pen-ar-Gúezec tourelles just to the right of les Trois Pierres tourelle. When abreast of Scaubeck turn for the quay.

There are several small fishing boats kept here and the best drying berth is alongside the west face of the quay, *5·3m*. The north side isn't up to much and the slip covers most of the south. There is a very adjacent café but it is $2\frac{1}{2}$km to the nearest village, Pleubian. A quiet corner for a *digestif* perhaps to round off a few of the seventy-five harbours all the way from Omonville. You are now at the most northerly point in Brittany, a natural halt to consider Part II—over a hundred more places between Port Blanc and Raz de Sein. Care to force down another cognac before going on?

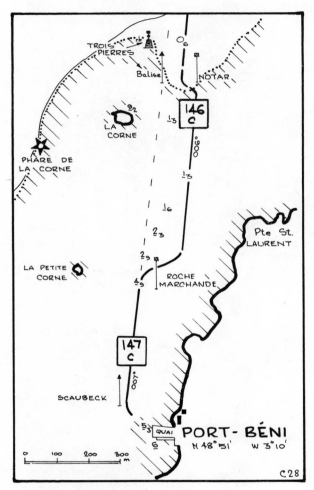

Chart C28—Port Béni

Index

Harbours, anchorages and approaches only are indexed.